1 MONTH OF
FREE
READING

at

www.ForgottenBooks.com

By purchasing this book you are eligible for one month membership to ForgottenBooks.com, giving you unlimited access to our entire collection of over 700,000 titles via our web site and mobile apps.

To claim your free month visit: www.forgottenbooks.com/free252962

ISBN 978-0-484-13723-2
PIBN 10252962

AMERICAN

HISTORICAL ASSOCIATION

OFFICERS

COMMITTEES

ACT OF INCORPORATION

CONSTITUTION

LIST OF MEMBERS

February, 1907

N. B. —Corrections in this list, and additions to it, especially as regards full names, academic degrees, and official positions held by members, should be sent to the Secretary.

Any member of this Association has the right to propose new names.

Nominations for membership in the Association should be addressed to the Secretary.

PRESS OF
KOHN & POLLOCK, INC.,
BALTIMORE.

AMERICAN HISTORICAL ASSOCIATION.

Members are hereby informed that the Association will have no copies of Volume II of the Annual Report for 1905 for distribution. The work comprises a Bibliography of American Historical Societies, by A. P. C. Griffin, forming a volume of about 1100 pages, in which is repeated and brought to date the Bibliography printed in the Association's Report for 1895.

Members desiring the volume may obtain it direct from the Public Printer, Washington, D. C., as provided by law, upon payment of cost of presswork and paper plus ten per cent. It is expected that the volume will be completed by June 1.

A. Howard Clark,
Secretary.

Washington, *March* 13, 1907.

AMERICAN HISTORICAL ASSOCIATION

Organized at Saratoga, N. Y., Sept. 10, 1884. Incorporated by Congress Jan. 4, 1889.

OFFICERS FOR 1907.

PRESIDENT

JOHN FRANKLIN JAMESON, Ph. D., LL. D.,
Carnegie Institution of Washington.

VICE-PRESIDENTS

GEORGE BURTON ADAMS, Ph. D., Litt. D.,
Professor Yale University.
ALBERT BUSHNELL HART, Ph. D., LL. D.,
Professor Harvard University.

SECRETARY AND CURATOR

A. HOWARD CLARK, A. M.,
Smithsonian Institution, Washington, D. C.

CORRESPONDING SECRETARY

CHARLES H. HASKINS, Ph. D.,
Professor Harvard University.

TREASURER

CLARENCE WINTHROP BOWEN, Ph. D.,
130 Fulton St., New York.

EXECUTIVE COUNCIL

In Addition to Above-Named Officers

(Ex-Presidents.)
ANDREW DICKSON WHITE, L. H. D., LL. D.,
Ithaca, N. Y.
JAMES SCHOULER, LL. D.,
Boston, Mass.
JAMES BURRILL ANGELL, LL. D.,
President University of Michigan.
GEORGE PARK FISHER, D. D., LL. D.,
Professor Yale University.
HENRY ADAMS, LL. D.,
Washington, D. C.
JAMES FORD RHODES, LL. D.,
Boston, Mass.
CHARLES' FRANCIS ADAMS, LL. D.,
Boston, Mass.

TERMS OF OFFICE

Deceased officers are marked thus †

Ex-Presidents

ANDREW DICKSON WHITE, L. H. D., LL. D., 1884-85.

†GEORGE BANCROFT, LL. D., 1885-86.

†JUSTIN WINSOR, LL. D., 1886-87.

†WILLIAM FREDERICK POOLE, LL. D., 1887-88.

†CHARLES KENDALL ADAMS, LL. D., 1888-89.

†JOHN JAY, LL. D., 1889-90.

†WILLIAM WIRT HENRY, LL. D., 1890-91.

JAMES BURRILL ANGELL, LL. D., 1891-93.

HENRY ADAMS, LL. D., 1893-94.

†GEORGE FRISBIE HOAR, LL. D., 1894-95.

†RICHARD SALTER STORRS, D. D., LL. D., 1895-96.

JAMES SCHOULER, LL. D., 1896-97.

GEORGE PARK FISHER, D. D., LL. D., 1897-98.

JAMES FORD RHODES, LL. D., 1898-99.

†EDWARD EGGLESTON, L. H. D., 1899-1900.

CHARLES FRANCIS ADAMS, LL. D., 1900-1901.

ALFRED THAYER MAHAN, D. C. L., LL. D., 1901-1902.

HENRY CHARLES LEA, LL. D., 1902-1903.

GOLDWIN SMITH, D. C. L., LL. D., 1903-1904.

JOHN BACH McMASTER, A. M., Ph. D., Litt. D., LL. D., 1904-1905.

SIMEON E. BALDWIN, LL. D., 1905-1906.

Ex-Vice-Presidents

†JUSTIN WINSOR, LL. D., 1884-86.

†CHARLES KENDALL ADAMS, LL. D., 1884-88.

†WILLIAM FREDERICK POOLE, LL. D., 1886-87.

†JOHN JAY, LL. D., 1887-89.

†WILLIAM WIRT HENRY, LL. D., 1888-90.

JAMES BURRILL ANGELL, LL. D., 1889-91.

HENRY ADAMS, LL. D., 1890-93.

†EDWARD GAY MASON, A. M., 1891-93.

†GEORGE FRISBIE HOAR, LL. D., 1893-94.

†RICHARD SALTER STORRS, D. D., LL. D., 1894-95.

JAMES SCHOULER, LL. D., 1894-96.

GEORGE PARK FISHER, D. D., LL. D., 1896-97.

JAMES FORD RHODES, LL. D., 1896-98.

†EDWARD EGGLESTON, L. H. D., 1898-99.

†MOSES COIT TYLER, L. H. D., LL. D., 1897-1900.

CHARLES FRANCIS ADAMS, LL. D., 1899-1900.

†HERBERT BAXTER ADAMS, Ph. D., LL. D., 1900-1901.

ALFRED THAYER MAHAN, D. C. L., LL. D., 1900-1901.

GOLDWIN SMITH, D. C. L., LL. D., 1901-1903.

†EDWARD McCRADY, LL. D., 1902-1903.

JOHN BACH McMASTER, LL. D., 1903-1904.

SIMEON E. BALDWIN, LL. D., 1904-1905.

J. FRANKLIN JAMESON, Ph. D., LL. D., 1905-1906.

COMMITTEES—1907

ANNUAL COMMITTEES.

COMMITTEE ON PROGRAM FOR THE TWENTY-SECOND AN-NUAL MEETING (Madison, 1907): A. L. P. Dennis, Charles H. Haskins, F. H. Hodder, Frederick J. Turner, Andrew C. McLaughlin, C. H. Van Tyne.

JOINT LOCAL COMMITTEE OF ARRANGEMENTS FOR THE AMERICAN HISTORICAL ASSOCIATION, THE AMERICAN ECONOMIC ASSOCIATION, THE AMERICAN POLITICAL SCIENCE ASSOCIATION AND THE AMERICAN SOCIOLOGICAL SOCIETY: Burr W. Jones, Richard T. Ely, Carl R. Fish, Dana C. Munro, Paul C. Reinsch, Edward A. Ross, R. G. Thwaites, William F. Vilas.

RECEPTION COMMITTEE OF LADIES: Mrs. Lucius Fairchild, Mrs. William F. Allen, Miss Ida M. Tarbell.

CONFERENCE OF STATE AND LOCAL HISTORICAL SOCIETIES: Frank H. Severance, Chairman; Evarts B. Greene, Secretary.

STANDING COMMITTEES, COMMISSIONS AND BOARDS.

EDITORS OF THE AMERICAN HISTORICAL REVIEW: J. Franklin Jameson, William F. Sloane, Albert Bushnell Hart, George L. Burr (these five hold over); George B. Adams, re-elected for term ending January 1, 1913.

HISTORICAL MANUSCRIPTS COMMISSION: J. Franklin Jameson, Edward G. Bourne, Frederick W. Moore, Worthington C. Ford, Thomas M. Owen, James A. Woodburn.

COMMITTEE ON THE JUSTIN WINSOR PRIZE: Charles H. Hull, Edward P. Cheyney, Williston Walker, Evarts B. Greene, J. H. Latane.

COMMITTEE ON THE HERBERT BAXTER ADAMS PRIZE: Charles Gross, George L. Burr, Victor Coffin, John Martin Vincent, James W. Thompson. (During the absence of Professor Gross in Europe after June 1, 1907, Professor Burr will act as chairman of the committee).

PUBLIC ARCHIVES COMMISSION: Herman V. Ames, Herbert L. Osgood, Charles M. Andrews, Dunbar Rowland, Robert. T. Swan, Clarence S. Brigham, Carl R. Fish.

COMMITTEE ON BIBLIOGRAPHY: Ernest C. Richardson, A. P. C. Griffin, William C. Lane, S. H. Siebert, V. H. Paltsits, James T. Shotwell.

ACT OF INCORPORATION

Be it enacted by the Senate and House of Representatives of the United States of America in Congress assembled, That Andrew D. White, of Ithaca, in the State of New York; George Bancroft, of Washington in the District of Columbia; Justin Winsor, of Cambridge, in the State of Massachusetts; William F. Poole, of Chicago, in the State of Illinois; Herbert B. Adams, of Baltimore, in the State of Maryland; Clarence W. Bowen, of Brooklyn, in the State of New York; their associates and successors, are hereby created, in the District of Columbia a body corporate and politic by the name of the American Historical Association for the promotion of historical studies, the collection and preservation of historical manuscripts, and for kindred purposes in the interest of American history and of history in America. Said Association is authorized to hold real and personal estate in the District of Columbia so far only as may be necessary to its lawful ends to an amount not exceeding five hundred thousand dollars, to adopt a constitution, and make by-laws not inconsistent with law. Said Association shall have its principal office at Washington, in the District of Columbia, and may hold its annual meetings in such places as the said incorporators shall determine. Said Association shall report annually to the Secretary of the Smithsonian Institution concerning its proceedings and the condition of historical study in America. Said Secretary shall communicate to Congress the whole of such reports, or such portions thereof as he shall see fit. The Regents of the Smithsonian Institution are authorized to permit said Association to deposit its collections, manuscripts, books, pamphlets, and other material for history in the Smithsonian Institution or in the National Museum at their discretion, upon such conditions and under such rules as they shall prescribe.

[Approved, January 4, 1889.]

CONSTITUTION

I.

The name of this Society shall be THE AMERICAN HISTORICAL ASSOCIATION.

II.

Its object shall be the promotion of historical studies.

III.

Any person approved by the Executive Council may become a member by paying three dollars; and after the first year may continue a member by paying an annual fee of three dollars. On payment of fifty dollars, any person may become a life-member exempt from fees. Persons not resident in the United States may be elected as honorary or corresponding members, and be exempt from the payment of fees.

IV.

The officers shall be a President, two Vice-Presidents, a Secretary, a Corresponding Secretary, a Curator, a Treasurer, and an Executive Council consisting of the foregoing officers and six other members elected by the Association with the Ex-Presidents of the Association. These officers shall be elected by ballot at each regular annual meeting of the Association.

V.

The Executive Council shall have charge of the general interests of the Association, including the election of members, the calling of meetings, the selection of papers to be read, and the determination of what papers shall be published.

VI.

This Constitution may be amended at any annual meeting, notice of such amendment having been given at the previous annual meeting, or the proposed amendment having received the approval of the Executive Council.

LIST OF MEMBERS
OF THE
AMERICAN HISTORICAL ASSOCIATION

HONORARY MEMBER

BRYCE, RT. HON. JAMES, P. C., D. C. L., LL. D., F. R. S., Washington, D. C.

ABBE, MRS. ROBERT, President of the City History Club of New York, 11 W. 50th St., New York, N. Y.

ABBOTT, MISS IDA, Fairmont State Normal School, 227 High St., Fairmont, West Va. .

ABBOTT, MISS KATHARINE M., 24 Fairmount St., Lowell, Mass.

ABBOTT, LYMAN, D. D., LL. D., 287 Fourth Ave., New York.

ABBOTT, OSMER, A. B., Ph. D., Principal Washington Union High School, Oleander, Cal. (Pacific Coast Branch.)

ABBOTT, WILBUR CORTEZ, B. A., M. A. B. Litt. (Oxon.), Professor of European History, University of Kansas, Lawrence, Kan.

ABEL, ANNA HELOISE, A. B., A. M., Ph. D., The Woman's College of Baltimore, Baltimore, Md.

ABELSON, PAUL, DeWitt Clinton High School, 500 W. 59th St., New York, N. Y.

ADAMS, MISS ALICE DANA, A. M., 93 Hancock St., Auburndale, Mass

ADAMS, ARLON TAYLOR, A. M., Tilton Seminary, Tilton, N. H.

*ADAMS, CHARLES FRANCIS, LL. D., President Massachusetts Historical Society, 23 Court St., Boston, Mass.

ADAMS, EPHRAIM DOUGLASS, Ph. D., Stanford University, Cal. (Pacific Coast Branch.)

ADAMS, PROF. FRANK YALE, A. M., 1043 Florida St., Los Angeles, Cal. (Pacific Coast Branch.)

ADAMS, GEORGE BURTON, Ph. D., Litt. D., Professor Yale University, New Haven, Conn.

ADAMS, GEORGE E., 530 Belden Ave., Chicago, Ill.

* Life members.

*ADAMS, HENRY, LL. D., 1603 H St., Washington, D. C.

ADAMS, HENRY CARTER, LL. D., Professor University of Michigan, Ann Arbor, Mich.

ADAMS, JOSEPH, Lakota Hotel, Chicago, Ill.

ADAMS, MISS MARY D., A. B., 76 Pearl St., Middletown, Conn.

ADAMS, MISS VICTORIA A., A. B., 443 East 56th St., Chicago, Ill.

ADLER, CYRUS, Ph. D., Assistant Secretary Smithsonian Institution, Washington, D. C.

AERY, WILLIAM ANTHONY, A. M., Hampton Institute, Hampton, Va.

AIMES, HUBERT H. S., Ph. B., Ph. D., College of the City of New York, New York, N. Y.

AINSWORTH, HARRY, Moline, Ill.

AINSWORTH, JAMES EDWARD, B. S., C. E., 1728 Fifth Ave., Moline, Ill.

ALBERT, MISS GRACE, care T. B. Browne, Wynnewood, Pa.

ALDEN, GEORGE HENRY, Ph. D., Professor University of Washington, Seattle, Wash. (Pacific Coast Branch.)

ALDERSON, MRS. PERSIS HURD, Ph. M., Professor Upper Iowa University, Fayette, Iowa.

ALDRICH, CHARLES, Historical Department of Iowa, Des Moines, Iowa.

ALEXANDER, ROBERT OWEN, Esq., 23 East Fourth St., Charlotte, N. C.

ALEXIUS, SISTER MARY, O. S. D., St. Clara College, Sinsinawa, Wis.

ALGER, JOHN LINCOLN, A. M., Principal Vermont Academy, Saxtons River, Vt.

ALLEN, ANDREW HUSSEY, A. B., Kingston, R. I.

ALLEN, CHARLES L., 23 Portland Block, Chicago, Ill.

ALLEN, MISS FREDONIA, Ph. B., Principal Tudor Hall School for Girls, 1530 N. Meridian St., Indianapolis, Ind.

ALLEN, GARDNER WELLS, A. B., M. D., 419 Boylston St., Boston, Mass.

ALLEN, JOSEPH DANA, A. M., Delancey School, 1420 Pine St., Philadelphia, Pa.

ALLISON, WILLIAM HENRY, Ph. D., Professor of History and Political Science at Franklin College, Franklin, Ind.

ALVORD, CLARENCE W., University of Illinois, 1101 California Ave., Urbana, Ill.

AMBLER, CHARLES HENRY, West Virginia University, Morgantown, W. Va.

*AMEN, HARLEN PAGE, A. M., Principal Phillips Exeter Academy, Exeter, N. H.

AMES, MAJ. AZEL, M. D., 24 Yale Ave., Wakefield, Mass.

AMES, CHARLES H., 120 Boylston St., Boston, Mass.

AMES, HERMAN VANDENBURG, Ph. D., Professor University of Pennsylvania, Philadelphia, Pa.

AMES, JAMES BARR, LL. D., Professor Harvard Law School, Cambridge, Mass.

AMORY, ARTHUR, A. M., 133 Marlborough St., Boston, Mass.

ANDERSON, ARCHIBALD B., Principal High School, Colusa, Cal.

ANDERSON, BELLE B., A. B., The Misses Master School, Dobbs Ferry, N. Y.

ANDERSON, C. N., State Normal School, Kearney, Neb.

ANDERSON, D. R., A. M., President of Willie Halsell College, Vinita, Ind. Ter.

ANDERSON, FRANK MALOY, A. M., Assistant Professor of History, University of Minnesota, 1629 University Ave., S. E., Minneapolis, Minn.

ANDERSON, MRS. JAMES T., 1421 Wood Ave., Colorado Springs, Colo.

ANDERSON, JOSEPH, D. D., Woodmont, Conn.

ANDERSON, LUTHER, 310 York St., New Haven, Conn.

ANDIS, ELIJAH S., University of Kansas, Lawrence, Kansas.

ANDOVER THEOLOGICAL SEMINARY LIBRARY, Andover, Mass.

ANDREWS, ARTHUR I., 253 Broadway, Providence, R. I.

ANDREWS, CHARLES McLEAN, Ph. D., Professor Bryn Mawr College, Bryn Mawr, Pa.

ANDREWS, GEORGE FREDERICK, A. M., 4 Young Orchard Ave., Providence, R. I.

ANDREWS, MARTIN R., Professor of History and Political Science, Marietta College, Marietta, Ohio.

ANDREWS, WILLIAM GIVEN, D. D., President of Trustees of Henry Whitfield House, State Historical Museum, Guilford, Conn.

ANGELL, JAMES BURRILL, LL. D., President University of Michigan, Ann Arbor, Mich.

ANJOU, GUSTAVE, Ph. D., Hasbrouck Heights, N. J.

ANTHOINE, EDWARD S., A. B., M. A., 57 Exchange St., Portland, Me.

ARMITAGE, A. WESLEY, Superintendent of Schools, Plankinton, S. D.

ARMOUR, GEORGE ALLISON, A. M., Princeton, N. J.

ARMSTRONG, EDWIN E., 128 Jefferson Ave., Detroit, Mich.

ARMSTRONG, HENRY I., 130 Jefferson Ave., Detroit, Mich.

ARNDT, WALTER TALLMADGE, A. M., Harvard Club, 27 W. 44th St., New York, N. Y.

ARNOLD, REV. CHARLES LOUDON, A. M., Detroit, Mich.

ARNOLD, GEORGE F., 81 Davis Ave., Brookline, Mass.

ARNOLD, GEORGE S., B. A., 24 Dwight St., New Haven, Conn.

ARNOLD, JAMES N., 10 Foster St., P. O. Box 114, Providence, R. I.

ARNOLD, MOTT H., Eugene, Ore. (Pacific Coast Branch.)

ASAKAWA, K., Dartmouth College, Hanover, N. H.

ASHBROOK, JOSEPH, 3614 Baring St., Philadelphia, Pa.

ASHBY, AUBREY LEONARD, Olivet, Mich.

ASHLEY, ROSCOE L., 95 S. Madison Ave., Los Angeles, Cal.

*ATHERTON, MRS. GERTRUDE, care The Macmillan Company, New York, N. Y.

ATWATER, MRS. HARRIET STARK CHASE, Fowler Building, Suite 1, Concord, N. H.

AUSTIN, HATTIE, 1210 4th St., S. E., Minneapolis, Minn.

AUSTIN, JAMES, JR., A. M., 503 National Union Bldg., Toledo, Ohio.

AUTRY, JAMES L., Beaumont, Texas.

AVERILL, MISS MARY AUGUSTA, A. B., 379 Harvard St., Cambridge, Mass.

AVERY, ELIZABETH HUNTINGTON, Ph. D., Professor of English and History, Redfield College, Redfield, S. Dakota.

AVERY, HON. ELROY MCKENDREE, Ph. D., LL. D., 2831 Woodhill Road, S. E., Cleveland, O.

AVERY, ENOCH THADDEUS, Croton Falls, N. Y.

*AYER, EDWARD E., 1515 Railway Exchange Building, Chicago, Ill.

AYER, JOHN FRANCIS, President Somerville Historical Society, 213 Lowell St., Wakefield, Mass.

AYER, JOSEPH CULLEN, Jr., Ph. D., Divinity School, 5000 Woodland Ave., Philadelphia, Pa.

AYER, MELVILLE C., Biddeford, Me.

AYLSWORTH, LEON EMMONS, A. B., 2048 Vine St., Lincoln, Neb.

AYRAULT, GUY, ESQ., Groton School, Groton Mass.

BABB, JAMES ELISHA, B. S., LL. B., Lewiston, Idaho. (Pacific Coast Branch.)

BABCOCK, EARLE BROWNELL, Ph. B., University of Chicago, 307 East 56th St., Chicago, Ill.

BABCOCK, KENDRIC CHARLES, Ph. D., President University of Arizona, Tucson, Ariz. (Pacific Coast Branch.)

BABINE, ALEXIS VASILIEVICH, A. M., Associated Press, 39 Galernga, St. Petersburg, Russia.

BACON, EDGAR MAYHEW, Tarrytown, N. Y.

BACON, MRS. GEORGE WOOD, 23 West 67th St., New York, N. Y.

BACON, LEON BROOKS, B. A., LL. B., 907 Williamson Building, Cleveland, Ohio.

BACON, PAUL VALENTINE, A. B., 378 Wabash Ave., Chicago, Ill.

BACON, THOMAS R., Professor University of California, Berkeley, Cal. (Pacific Coast Branch.)

BAGLEY, CLARENCE B., President, Washington University, State Historical Society, Seattle, Wash. (Pacific Coast Branch.)

BAILEY, CHARLOTTE O., 4756 Kenwood Ave., Chicago, Ill.

BAIN, JAMES, D. C. L., Chief Librarian Public Library, Toronto, Ont., Canada.

BAIRMAN, WILLIAM M., The Macon Telegraph, Macon, Ga.

BAKER, ALFRED LANDON, Lake Forest, Ill.

BAKER, GEORGE ALBERT, Secretary Northern Indiana Historical Society, 102 S. Michigan St., South Bend, Ind.

BALCH, ELIZABETH, Head of History Dept., St. Agnes School, Albany, N. Y.

BALCH, ERNEST A., Ph. D., 614 Hammond Building, Detroit, Mich.

*BALCH, THOMAS WILLING, A. B., LL. B., 1412 Spruce St., Philadelphia, Pa.

BALDWIN, MISS ALICE M., The Baldwin School, Bryn Mawr, Pa.

BALDWIN, MISS BLANCHE, High School for Girls, 438 N. 33d St., Philadelphia, Pa.

BALDWIN, ERNEST HICKOK, M. A., Ph. D., 448 Saranac Lake, N. Y.

BALDWIN, JAMES FOSDICK, Ph. D., 289 Mill St., Poughkeepsie, N. Y.

BALDWIN, ROBERT R., 107 Dearborn St., Chicago, Ill.

*BALDWIN, HON. SIMEON EBEN, LL. D., Professor of Constitutional Law, Yale University; Associate Judge of Supreme Court of Errors of Conn., 69 Church St., New Haven, Conn.

BALL, HON. DAN HARVEY, Marquette, Mich.

BALLAGH, JAMES CURTIS, Ph. D., Johns Hopkins University, Baltimore, Md.

BALLOU, HOSEA STARR, Brookline, Mass.

BANCROFT, FREDERIC, Ph. D., LL. D., 1700 H St., Washington, D. C.

*BANCROFT, HUBERT HOWE, A. M., San Francisco, Cal.

BANKS, MISS MARY, Seattle Public Library, Seattle, Wash.

BANTA, THEODORE MELVIN, 144 St. James Place, Brooklyn, N. Y.

BARBOUR, LEVI LEWIS, A. M., 30 Buhl Block, Detroit, Mich.

BARHYDT, REV. GEORGE WEED, New Milford, Conn.

BARKER, EUGENE CAMPBELL, M. A., University of Texas, Austin, Texas.

BARNARD, JOB, Associate Justice of the Supreme Court of the District of Columbia, 1306 Rhode Island Ave. N. W., Washington, D. C.

BARNES, HENRY, M. D., New England Bldg., Cleveland, Ohio.

BARNETT, JAMES F., 126 N. Lafayette St., Grand Rapids, Mich.

BARNUM, WILLIAM MILO, A. B., LL. B., 62 Cedar St., New York, N. Y.

BARR, HESTER A., 6422 Eggleston Ave., Chicago, Ill.

BARRETT, JOSEPH HARTWELL, Park Place, Loveland, Ohio.

BARROWS, CAROLINE L., 633 Western Ave., Connersville, Ind.

BARSTOW, CHARLES L., A. B., 34 Gramercy Park, New York, N. Y.

BARTHOLOMAY, HENRY, JR., 28 Portland Block, Chicago, Ill.

*Barton, EDMUND MILLS, Librarian American Antiquarian Society, Worcester, Mass.

BASS, BERTHA, A. M., Wadleigh High School, 114th St., near 7th Ave., New York, N. Y.

BASS, HORACE HERBERT, 416 West 11th St., Anderson, Ind.

BASSETT, AUSTIN BRADLEY, B. D., 133 Washington St., Hartford, Conn.

BASSETT, JOHN SPENCER, Ph. D., Professor Trinity College, President Trinity College Historical Society, Durham, N. C.

BATCHELLER, MRS. EMMA W., 55 Commonwealth Ave., Boston, Mass.

BATCHELLER, ROBERT, 55 Commonwealth Ave., Boston, Mass.

BATCHELOR, JAMES OTTERBEIN, Principal of Hoagland Schools, 231 West Butler St., Fort Wayne, Ind.

BATES, ABBY BARSTOW, A. M., Morris High School, 166th St. and Boston Road, New York, N. Y.

BATES, ALBERT CARLOS, Recording Secretary and Librarian Connecticut Historical Society, Hartford, Conn.

BATES, FRANK GREENE, B. L., Ph. D., Professor Alfred University, Alfred, N. Y.

BATES, GEORGE WILLIAMS, A. B., A. M., 32 Buhl Building, Detroit, Mich.

BATTLE, KEMP PLUMMER, LL. D., Professor University of North Carolina, President North Carolina Historical Society, Chapel Hill, N. C.

BAUER, FREDERIC GILBERT, A. B., Vice-President Old South Historical Society, 20 Burroughs St., Jamaica Plain, Mass.

BAUSMAN, REV. JOSEPH H., A. M., Rochester, Pa.

BAXTER, JAMES PHINNEY, A. M., Litt. D., President Maine Historical Society, and New England Historic Genealogical Society, Member of Council American Antiquarian Society, Portland, Me.

BAYLOR, MISS ADELAIDE STEELE, Ph. B., Superintendent City Schools, Wabash, Ind.

BEACH, MYRON HAWLEY, A. B., LL. D., 404 The Rookery, 217 La Salle St., Chicago, Ill.

BEACH, WALTER G., The State College of Washington, Pullman, Wash. (Pacific Coast Branch.)

BEACH, WILLIAM HARRISON, A. M., Seneca Falls, N. Y.

BEALE, JOSEPH HENRY, JR., LL. D., Professor of Law, Harvard University, Cambridge, Mass.

BEAN, ROBERT S., 130 East 11th St., Eugene, Ore. (Pacific Coast Branch.)

BEANSTON, GEORGE, 542 Steiner St., San Francisco, Cal. (Pacific Coast Branch).

BEARD, DR. CHARLES A., Columbia University, New York, N. Y.

BEARDSLEY, HARRY MERCHANT, Ph. B., 371 W. First St., Elmira, N. Y.

BEATMAN, AUGUSTUS S., Department of History, Polytechnic Preparatory School, Brooklyn, N. Y.

BEAUMONT, JOHN W., 60 Buhl Block, Detroit, Mich.

BECKER, CARL LOTUS, Assistant Professor European History, University of Kansas, Lawrence, Kan.

BECKWITH, MISS FRANCES A., 46 E. 21st St., New York.

BEEMAN, LARKIN LEWIS, A. B., 85 W. Mulbury St., Kokomo, Ind.

BEER, GEORGE LOUIS, A. M., 329 W. 71st St., New York.

BEER, WILLIAM, Librarian, Howard Memorial Library, and of New Orleans Free Public Library, New Orleans, La.

BEITLER, JUDGE ABRAHAM M., Room 231, City Hall, Philadelphia, Pa.

BELCHER, MISS KATHARINE FISHER, High School, Newark, N. J.

BELFIELD, HENRY HOLMES, A. M., Ph. D., 5738 Washington Ave., Chicago, Ill.

BELL, GEORGE WILLIAM, A. M., History Department, Olivet College, Olivet, Mich.

BELL, JOHN RANDOLPH, 3001 Osceola St., Denver, Colo.

BELT, ELIZABETH TALBOT, Millen, Ga.

BEMAN, LAMAR T., A. B., A. M., East High School, 29 McConnell St., Cleveland, Ohio.

BENBOW, LEE L., A. B., County Superintendent Pierce Co., 218 South I St., Tacoma, Wash.

BENJAMIN, GILBERT GIDDINGS, Ph. B., Yale University, New Haven, Conn.

BENNESON, MISS CORA AGNES, LL. B., A. M., 4 Mason St., Cambridge, Mass.

BENTON, ELBERT JAY, Ph. D., Western Reserve University, Cleveland, Ohio.

BENTON, JOSIAH HENRY, JR., A. M., Ames Building., Boston, Mass.

BERGER, PROFESSOR FERDINAND, A. M., Western University of Pennsylvania, Allegheny, Pa.

BERND, FLORENCE, A. B., Macon, Ga.

BERNHEIM, ISAAC WOLFE, 1108 3rd St., Louisville, Ky.

BESTOR, ARTHUR EUGENE, A. B., University of Chicago, Chicago, Ill.

BEYER, H. OTLEY, Bayombong, Province of Nueva Vizcaya, P. I.

BIBLIOTHEQUE DE L'UNIVERSITE. Caen (Calvador), France.

BIGELOW, MISS BLANCHE T., State University, Eugene, Ore. (Pacific Coast Branch.)

*BIGELOW, FRANK GORDON, Milwaukee, Wis.

BIGELOW, HENRY NELSON, 82 Monmouth St., Brookline, Mass.

BIGELOW, HON. JOHN, LL. D., Highland Falls, Orange Co., N. Y.

*BIGELOW, MELVILLE MADISON, Ph. D., LL. D., Dean of Boston University Law School, Ashburton Place, Boston, Mass.

*BIGELOW, POULTNEY, A. M., F. R. G. S., Boston, Mass.

BIGGAR, HENRY PERCIVAL, B. A., B. Litt., 15 Rue de Beaujolais, Paris, France.

BILLINGS, JOHN SHAW, LL. D., D. C. L. Director New York Public Library, New York, N. Y.

*BINGHAM, HIRAM, A. M., Hill House, Reservoir St., Cambridge, Mass.

BIRD, HON. HARLAN PAGE, Wausaukee, Wis.

BISBEE, MARVIN DAVIS, A. B., B. D., Librarian Dartmouth College Library, Hanover, N. H.

BISHOP, ARTHUR G., B. S., Flint, Mich.

*BISHOP, CORTLANDT F., A. M., Ph. D., LL. B., Room 1410, 52 William St., New York, N. Y.

BISHOP, JOSEPH T., A. B., 38 Divinity Hall, Cambridge, Mass.

BISHOP, THOMAS B., 2309 Washington St., San Francisco, Calif. (Pacific Coast Branch.)

BISHOP, WILLIAM WARNER, Library of Princeton University, Princeton, N. J.

BISSELL, JOHN HENRY, A. M., 80 Griswold St., Detroit, Mich.

BISSET, CHARLES, A. M., Campbell College, Holton, Kan.

BIXBY, WILLIAM K., Northeast corner Kings Highway and Lindell Ave., St. Louis, Mo.

BIXLER, WILLIAM SHELTON, Ph. M., Owensville, Ind.

BLACK, JAMES CHURCHILL, Ph. D., 304 13th St., W., Anderson, Ind.

BLACK, JAMES WILLIAM, Ph. D., Professor Colby College, Waterville, Maine.

BLACKMAN, MISS ELMA M., 809 S. Rose St., Kalamazoo, Mich.

BLACKMAR, FRANK WILSON, Ph. D., Professor University of Kansas, Lawrence, Kan.

BLAIR, MISS EMMA HELEN, A. M., State Historical Library, Madison, Wis.

BLAIR, JOHN HAMILTON, A. M., Llenroe, Ithaca, N. Y.

BLAIR, MONTGOMERY, Room 7, Corcoran Bldg., Washington, D. C.

BLAIR, WILLIAM P., East Des Moines High School, 1126 6th Ave., Des Moines, Iowa.

BLAKESLEE, GEORGE H., Ph. D., Assistant Professor of History, Clark College, Worcester, Mass.

BLANCHARD, MISS ELLEN CAROLINE, High School, 70 Thorn St., Massillon, Ohio.

BLANCHARD, NATHAN W., Santa Paula, Calif. (Pacific Coast Branch.)

BLATCHFORD, ELIPHALET WICKES, A. B., LL. D., 375 La Salle Ave., Chicago, Ill.

BLATCHFORD, PAUL, A. B., 433 N. Euclid Ave., Oak Park, Ill.

BLAUVELT, MARY TAYLOR, 117 5th Ave., W., Roselle, N. J.

*BLISS, EUGENE FREDERICK, A. M., 450 E. 5th St., Cincinnati, Ohio.

BLISS, WILBERFORCE, B. S., B. L., State Normal School, San Diego, Calif. (Pacific Coast Branch.)

BLOCHMAN, MRS. IDA MAY, High School, Santa Maria, Cal. (Pacific Coast Branch.)

BLOCK, WILLARD F., 100 Washington St., Chicago, Ill.

BLODGETT, JAMES HARVEY, A. M., 1229 N St., N. W., Washington, D. C.

BLOOMSTEIN, MISS LIZZIE L., A. M., Peabody College for Teachers, 521 S. Summer St., Nashville, Tenn.

BODE, ESTELLE REGNIA, 4230 Langland St., Cincinnati, Ohio.

BOGARDUS, FRANK SMITH, A. B., Professor of European History, Indiana State Normal School, Terre Haute, Ind.

BOGLE, THOMAS ASHFORD, Professor University of Michigan, Ann Arbor, Mich.

BOHN, FRANK ARTHUR, Ph. D., care W. E. Bohn, University of Michigan, Ann Arbor, Mich.

BOIES, MISS BESSIE, B. A., 5833 Monroe Ave., Chicago, Ill.

BOLLES, EDWIN CORTLAND, Ph. D., D. D., Professor Tufts College, Tufts College, Mass.

BOLTON, HERBERT E., Ph. D., University of Texas, Austin, Texas.

BONAPARTE, CHARLES JOSEPH, LL. B., Baltimore, Md.

BOND, BEVERLY W., JR., Clarksville, Tenn.

BOND, JUDGE JAMES ALEXANDER CHESLEY, Westminster, Md.

BOOK, JAMES B., M. D., Detroit, Mich.

BOOTH, PERCY NEWHALL, Kenyon Bldg., 216 5th St., Louisville, Ky.

BOOTH, WILLIAM STONE, 4 Park St., Boston, Mass.

BORLAND, MRS. JOHN JAY, 2027 Prairie Ave., Chicago, Ill.

BOSLEY, WILLIAM BRADFORD, 925 Franklin St., San Francisco, Cal. (Pacific Coast Branch.)

BOSTON COLLEGE, The President of, Boston, Mass.

BOTSFORD, GEORGE WILLIS, Ph. D., Columbia University, New York, N. Y.

BOURLAND, BENJAMIN PARSONS, Ph. D., 2662 Euclid Ave., Cleveland, O.

BOURLAND, OGDEN PHELPS, Pontiac, Ill.

BOURNE, ANNIE R., A. B., Bethany College, Bethany, West Va.

BOURNE, EDWARD GAYLORD, Ph. D., Professor Yale University, New Haven, Conn.

BOURNE, HENRY ELDRIDGE, B. D., Professor Cleveland College for Women, Western Reserve University, Cleveland, Ohio.

*BOWDOIN, GEORGE S., 39 Park Ave., New York, N. Y.

*BOWEN, CLARENCE WINTHROP, Ph. D., Treasurer American Historical Association, 130 Fulton St., New York, N. Y.

BOWMAN, H. M., Ph. D. (22 Church St.), Berlin, Ontario, Canada.

BOWMAN, JACOB N., Ph. D., Professor of History, State Normal School, Whatcom, Wash. (Pacific Coast Branch.)

BOYD, WILLIAM KENNETH, Ph. D., Trinity College, Durham, N. C.

BOYLE, E. MORTIMER, LL. B., 179 W. 88th St., New York, N. Y.

*BRACKETT, JEFFREY RICHARDSON, Ph. D., 41 Marlborough St., Boston, Mass.

BRADEN, JAMES ANDREW, Thoreau St., Lakewood, Cleveland, Ohio.

BRADFORD, JOHN EWING, Miami University, Oxford, Ohio.

BRADLEY, COL. J. PAYSON, 24 Purchase St., Boston, Mass.

BRADLEY, MARIE M., 514 Lake St., Madison,Wis. (Pacific Coast Branch.)

BRAMHALL, MISS EDITH CLEMENTINE, A. M., Ph. D., Professor of History, Rockford College, Rockford, Ill.

BRANT, SELWYN A., Madison, Wis.

BRANTLY, WILLIAM THEOPHILUS, LL. B., 10 E. Fayette St., Baltimore, Md.

BRETT, HENRY, A. M., Calumet, Mich.

BRETZ, JULIEN P., Ph. D., Associate in History, University of Chicago, 6147 Minerva Ave., Chicago, Ill.

BREWER, JOHN A., 403 Craigie St., Cambridge, Mass.

BREWER, LUTHER A., Cedar Rapids, Iowa.

BREWER, MARGARET HALSEY, Woodley Inn, Cathedral Heights, Washington, D. C.

BREWER, THEODORE H., Wofford College, Spartansburg, S. C.

BREWER, REV. WILLIAM AUGUSTUS, A. B., B. D., San Mateo, Cal. (Pacific Coast Branch.)

BRIGGS, FRANK OBADIAH, 198 W. State St., Trenton, N. J.

BRIGHAM, CLARENCE SAUNDERS, A. B., 95 Waterman St., Providence, R. I.

BRIGHAM, HERBERT OLIN, Rhode Island State Library, Providence, R. I.

BRILHART, GEORGE OLIVER, New Windsor, Md.

BRINSMADE, JOHN CHAPIN, A. B., Principal of The Gunnery, Washington, Conn.

BRISTOL, EDWARD N., 29 W. 23rd St., New York, N. Y.

BRITTINGHAM, THOMAS E., 640 N. Henry St., Madison, Wis.

BRITTON, LEWIS HENRY, Manila, P. I. (Pacific Coast Branch.)

BRITTON, RAYMOND M., Lawrence, Calif.

BROCK, ROBERT ALONZO, Registrar Virginia Society Sons of the American Revolution, Richmond, Va.

BROCKWAY, WILLIAM STEVENS, 406 Milwaukee St., Milwaukee, Wis.

BROOKS, EUGENE C., Superintendent of Schools, Goldsboro, N. C.

BROOKS, SARAH C., Principal, Baltimore Teachers' Training School, Baltimore, Md.

BROOKS, JAMES WILSON, A. M., LL. B., Petersham, Mass.

BROSS, REV. FRANK W., University of Wyoming, Laramie, Wyo.

BROUN, MAJOR THOMAS L., 1017 Virginia St., Charleston, W. Va.

BROWN, ASHMUN NORRIS, Executive Department, Olympia, Wash.

BROWN, EDWARD OSGOOD, A. B., Judge of the Appellate Court of Illinois, 400 North State St., Chicago, Ill.

BROWN, EDWARD THOMAS, Ph. B., Wolcott, Wayne Co., N. Y.

BROWN, EDWIN HENRY, JR., Centerville, Md.

BROWN, HON. HENRY BILLINGS, LL. D., Washington, D. C.

BROWN, HENRY JOHN, 4 Trafalgar Square, London, W. C., England.

BROWN, HOWELL CHAMBERS, B. A., 120 N. El Molino Ave., Pasadena, Cal. (Pacific Coast Branch.)

BROWN, JESSE W. C., A. B., Superintendent Colon Public School, Colon, Mich.

*BROWN, JOHN MARSHALL, A. M., Portland, Me.

BROWN, MISS LOUISE FARGO, A. B., Teacher of History, Lafayette High School, 39 Ketchum Place, Buffalo, N. Y.

BROWN, MARSHALL STEWART, A. M., 219 Palisade Ave., Yonkers, N. Y.

BROWN, S. ALICE, 66 Marlborough St., Boston, Mass.

BROWN, WILLIAM GARROTT, A. M., Harvard Club, New York, N. Y.

BROWN, WILLIAM LISTON, 217 Dempster St., Evanston, Ill.

BROWN, RT. REV. WILLIAM MONTGOMERY, D. D., 1222 Scott St., Little Rock, Ark.

BROWNE, SQUIRE F., A. B., Director Correspondence School, Washington University, St. Louis, Mo.

BROWNE, WILLIAM FISKE, D. D., 704 Park Ave., Beloit, Wis.

BROWNING, CHARLES H., Ardmore P. O., Montgomery Co., Pa.

BROWNSON, PROF. MARY W., Pennsylvania College for Women, Pittsburgh, Pa.

BRUCE, PHILLIP ALEXANDER, Clarkton, Va.

BRUMBACK LIBRARY, Van Wert, Ohio.

BRUMMER, SIDNEY D., M. A., 1356 Madison Ave., New York, N. Y.

BRUSH, CHARLES FRANCIS, Ph. D., LL. D., Cleveland, Ohio.

BRUSH, JAMES CURTIS, Carbondale, Ill.

BRUSIE, CHARLES FREDERICK, A. M., Ossining, N. Y.

BRYANT, COLONEL CHARLES BENJAMIN, Martinsville, Va.

BRYANT, WILLIAM MCKENDREE, M. A., LL. D., Webster Grove (St. Louis), Mo.

BRYCE, REV. GEORGE, LL. D., Professor in Manitoba College, 189 Colony St., Winnipeg, Manitoba.

BRYN MAWR COLLEGE LIBRARY, Bryn Mawr, Pa.

BRYSON LIBRARY, Teachers College, Columbia University, New York, N. Y.

BUCHANAN, JAMES SHANNON, B. S., Professor University of Oklahoma, Norman, Oklahoma.

BUCK, SOLON J., 12-A Conant Hall, Cambridge, Mass.

BUCKNAM, KATE DENA, 1207 Rhode Island Ave., Washington, D. C.

BUELL, BERTHA G., Michigan State Normal College, 1 North Summit St., Ypsilanti, Mich.

BUFFALO HISTORICAL SOCIETY, Historical Bldg., Delaware Park, Buffalo, N. Y.

BUFFALO PUBLIC LIBRARY, Buffalo, N. Y.

BUKEY, ROBERTA MAGRUDER (Mrs. John S.), Vienna, Va.

BULLARD, FRANCIS, A. B., 3 Commonwealth Ave., Boston, Mass.

BUMP, CHARLES WEATHERS, A. B., News Editor, Baltimore News, Baltimore, Md.

BURGESS, JOHN W., Ph. D., LL. D., Professor Columbia University, New York, N. Y.

BURKS, MRS. RIA MOUNGER, Wesleyan College, Macon, Ga.

BURNETT, EDMUND CODY, Ph. D., Carnegie Institution, Washington, D. C.

BURNHAM, JOHN H., McLean County Historical Society, Bloomington, Ill.

BURNHAM, SMITH, State Normal School, West Chester, Pa.

BURNS, RALPH HOUGHTON, B. A., Milaca, Minn.

*BURR, GEORGE LINCOLN, LL. D., Litt. D., Professor Cornell University, Ithaca, N. Y.

BURRAGE, HENRY SWEETSER, D. D., Togus, Maine.

BURROWS, CHARLES WILLIAM, Cleveland, Ohio.

BURROWS, HON. GEORGE BAXTER, Madison, Wis.

BURT, MISS AMY MAUD, Mount Pleasant, Mich.

BURT, THOMAS GREGORY, A. M., Ph. D., Professor Park College, Parkville, Mo.

BURTON, CLARENCE MONROE, 27 Brainard St., Detroit, Mich.

BUTLER, ARTHUR PIERCE, Morristown School, Morristown, N. J.

*BUTLER, NICHOLAS MURRAY, Ph. D., LL. D., President Columbia University, New York, N. Y.

BUTTE FREE PUBLIC LIBRARY, Butte, Mont.

BUTTERFIELD, ORA ELMER, LL. B., Detroit, Mich.

BUTTERWORTH, WILLIAM, Moline, Ill.

BYRNES, MISS CLARA, Associate Professor Normal College of New York, New York, N. Y.

*CABELL, HON. JAMES ALSTON, B. Sc., C. E., M. E., Cammander Military Order of Froeign Wars (Va.), 410 E. Grace St., Richmond, Va.

CABOT, ARTHUR TRACY, M. D., A. M., 1 Marlborough St., Boston, Mass.

CADWALLADER, RICHARD McCALL, A. B., A. M., LL. B., 133 S. 12th St., Philadelphia, Pa.

CAIN, A. R., M. D., Cambridge, Ohio.

CALDWELL, HOWARD .WALTER, A. M., Professor University of Nebraska; Secretary Nebraska State Historical Society, Lincoln, Neb.

CALDWELL, JOSHUA W., Knoxville, Tenn.

CALIFORNIA STATE LIBRARY, Sacramento, Cal.

CALKINS, W. W., Eugene, Ore. (Pacific Coast Branch.)

CALLAHAN, JAMES MORTON, Ph. D., Professor of History and Political Science, West Virginia University, Morgantown, West Va.

CALLAN, ESTELLE FOLTS (Mrs. Frank D.), 1626 Jackson Boulevard, Chicago, Ill.

CAMERON, MRS. ANGUS, The Chelsea, 222 W. 23rd St., New York, and La Crosse, Wis.

CAMPBELL, JAMES OSCAR, A. M., D. D., Westminster College, New Wilmington, Pa.

CAMPBELL, P. L., A. B., President University of Oregon, Eugene, Oregon. (Pacific Coast Branch.)

CANFIELD, GEORGE L., 62 Moffatt Building, Detroit, Mich.

CANNON, HENRY LEWIN, Ph. D., Stanford University, Cal. (Pacific Coast Branch.)

CANNON, REV. JAMES, JR., M. A., D. D., Principal Blackstone Female Institute, Blackstone, Va.

CAREY, HON. HENRY DE WITT, 70 Beaver St., New York, N. Y.

CAREY, JOSEPH, D. D., Saratoga, N. Y.

CARHART, ELIZABETH M., 33 W. 84th St., New York, N. Y.

CARLSON, FRANK, 1469 Amsterdam Ave., New York, N. Y.

CARMEN, REV. AUGUSTUS S., Educational Secretary The Ohio Baptist Educational Society, Granville, Ohio.

CARNEGIE LIBRARY, Atlanta, Ga.

CARNEGIE LIBRARY, Pittsburgh, Pa.

CARNELL, LAURA H., A. B., Litt. D., The Temple College, Philadelphia, Pa.

CARPENTER, ALLEN HARMON, A. M., Kenilworth, Ill.

CARPENTER, FREDERICK IVES, 5533 Woodlawn Ave., Chicago, Ill.

CARPENTER, LEONORA E., Eastern High School, Baltimore, Md. ,

CARR, JAMES EDWARD, JR., 227 Law Building, Baltimore, Md.

*CARRINGTON, GEN. HENRY BEEBEE, LL. D., U. S. A., Hyde Park (near Boston), Mass.

CARROLL, BENAJAH HARVEY, JR., A. B., A. M., LL. B., Th. M., Th. D., Ph. D., Professor in History and Economics, Baylor University, Waco, Texas.

CARSON, LUELLA CLAY, Eugene, Ore. (Pacific Coast Branch.)

CARTER, CLARENCE E., 631 State St., Madison, Wis.

CARTER, JAMES MADISON GORE, M. D., Ph. D., Professor College of Physicians and Surgeons, Chicago, 219 Claytòn St., Waukegan, Ill.

CARTER, MISS M. C., St. Timothy's School, Catonsville, Md.

CARTER, MISS SALLY RANDOLPH, St. Timothy's School, Catonsville, Md.

CARTWRIGHT, MRS. CHARLOTTE M., 215 7th St., Portland, Ore. (Pacific Coast Branch.)

CARTWRIGHT, OTHO GRANDFORD, M. A., Horace Mann Schools, New York, N. Y.

CARY, CHARLES H., 501 Chamber of Commerce Building, Portland, Ore. (Pacific Coast Branch.)

CARYL, MISS CHRISTINE, 5804 Rosalie Court, Chicago, Ill.

CATHCART, WALLACE HUGH, care of The Burrows Brothers, Cleveland, Ohio.

CATTERALL, RALPH CHARLES HENRY, A. B., Ph. D., 5 Central Ave., Ithaca, N. Y.

CENTRAL COLLEGE, Fayette, Mo.

CESSNA, ORANGE H., A. M., D. D., Professor Iowa State College, Ames, Iowa.

CHADWICK, REAR ADMIRAL FRENCH ENSOR, U. S. Navy, Twin Oaks, Newport, R. I.

CHADWICK, STILLMAN PERCY ROBERTS, A. M., 24 Irving St., Cambridge, Mass.

CHAMBERLAIN, JOSEPH PERKINS, University Club, San Francisco, Cal. (Pacific Coast Branch.)

CHAMBERLAIN, GEN. JOSHUA L., LL. D., Portland, Me.

CHAMPNEY, MRS. ELIZABETH W., A. B., 33 West 67th St., New York, N. Y.

CHANCELLOR, WILLIAM E., M. A., Superintendent Public Schools, Washington, D. C.

CHANDLER, MISS KATHERINE, 113 Duncan St., San Francisco, Cal. (Pacific Coast Branch.)

CHANDLER, JULIAN ALVIN CARROLL, Ph. D., LL. D., Director Jamestown Exposition, Norfolk, Va.

CHANNING, EDWARD, Ph. D., Professor Harvard University, Cambridge, Mass.

CHAPIN, ROBERT COIT, A. M., Professor Beloit College, Beloit, Wis.

CHAPMAN, REV. EDWARD MORTIMER, St. Johnsbury, Vt.

CHAPMAN, MISS FRANCES ELIZABETH, Woodside, Long Island, N. Y.

CHAPMAN, JOHN A., A. M., Newberry, South Carolina.

CHASE, MRS. CLEVELAND, A. B., Richmond, Ind.

CHASE, GEORGE L., Hartford, Conn.

CHASE, COL. JULIUS MILTON, 416 Sixth St., N. W., Washington, D. C.

CHASE, MISS MABELLE, A. B., 28 Hancock St., Everett, Mass.

CHASE, SYDNEY, 346 Beacon St., Boston, Mass.

CHATFIELD-TAYLOR, HOBART CHATFIELD, B. S., Fellow of the Royal Geographical Society of England and an "Officer de l'Instruction Publique" in France, Fairlawn, Lake Forest, Ill.

CHENERY, WILLIAM LUDLOW, Ashland, Va.

CHENEY, MISS BLANCHE A., 34 Arlington St., Lowell, Mass.

CHENEY, RT. REV. CHARLES EDWARD, D. D., 2409 Michigan Ave., Chicago, Ill.

CHESLEY, MABEL L., A. B., 168 St. James Place, Brooklyn, N. Y.

CHEYNEY, EDWARD POTTS, A. M., Professor University of Pennsylvania, Philadelphia, Pa.

CHICAGO HISTORICAL SOCIETY, 142 Dearborn Ave., Chicago, Ill.

CHICAGO PUBLIC LIBRARY, Chicago, Ill.

CHILDERS, COL. STACEY, Clarksville, Tenn.

CHILDS, JOEL N., A. B., Superintendent Public Schools, Preston, Minn.

CHITTENDEN, CAPT. HIRAM MARTIN, U. S. Engineer Office, Seattle, Wash.

CHITWOOD, OLIVER PERRY, Mercer University, Macon, Ga.

CHRISTIE, FRANCIS ALBERT, A. B., Professor Theological School, Meadville, Pa.

CHUBB, MABEL M., 2245 Piedmont Ave., Berkeley, Cal.

*CHURCH, HARRY VICTOR, Ph. B., Principal J. Sterling Morton Township High School, Berwyn, Ill.

CHYNOWETH, MISS EDNA RUTH, High School, 140 W. Gorham St., Madison, Wis.

CITY LIBRARY ASSOCIATION, Springfield, Mass.

CLARE, ISRAEL SMITH, Lancaster, Pa.

CLARK, ALONZO HOWARD, A. M., Curator of History National Museum, Editor Smithsonian Institution, Washington, D. C.

CLARK, MISS BELLE F., Philadelphia Normal School for Girls, Philadelphia, Pa.

CLARK, EMANUEL M., Ferris Institute, Big Rapids, Mich.

CLARK, EUGENE FRANCIS, 379 Central St., Auburndale, Mass.

CLARK, HERBERT W., Assistant in History, University of Michigan, Ann Arbor, Mich.

CLARK, REV. JOSEPH B., D. D., Fourth Ave. and 22nd St., New York, N. Y.

CLARK, LOTTA A., Charlestown High School, Boston, Mass.

CLARK, OLYNTHUS B., A. M., Professor of History Drake University, Des Moines, Iowa.

CLARK, ORLANDO E., Appleton, Wis.

CLARK, PROF. ROBERT CARLTON, A. M., Professor of History State Normal School, Bloomsburg, Pa.

CLEVELAND, MISS CATHERINE C., The Girls' Latin School, Baltimore, Md.

CLEVELAND, FREDERICK A., Ph. D., Professor of Finance (School of Commerce, Accounts and Finance, New York University), 30 Broad St., New York, N. Y.

*CLEVELAND, HON. GROVER, LL. D., Princeton, N. J.

CLEVELAND PUBLIC LIBRARY, Cleveland, Ohio.

CLOSE, MISS FRANCES HOBBY, Croton Falls, N. Y.

CLOTHIER, CLARKSON, 8th and Market Sts., Philadelphia, Pa.

COCHRANE, LAURA CAROLINE, M. E., 322 N. Maple Ave., Greensburg, Pa.

COCKE, WILLIAM IRBY, M. D., Port Washington, N. Y.

CODDING, JOHN WESLEY, A. M., Towanda, Pa.

COE, EDWARD BENTON, D. D., LL. D., 42 W. 52nd St., New York.

COEN, BENJAMIN FRANKLIN, Colorado Agricultural College, Fort Collins, Colo.

COES, MISS MARY, A. M., Radcliffe College, Cambridge, Mass.

COFFEEN, M. LESTER, 205 La Salle St., Chicago, Ill.

COFFIN, CHARLES P., Longwood, Brookline, Mass.

COFFIN, VICTOR, Ph. D., Professor University of Wisconsin, Madison, Wis.

COHEN, MENDES, President Maryland Historical Society, 825 N. Charles St., Baltimore. Md.

COHN, MORRIS M., Little Rock, Arkansas.

COIT, George W., M. D., Missouri Valley, Iowa.

COIT, MISS RUTH, 21 Chauncey St., Cambridge, Mass.

COKER, FRANCIS W., Livingston Hall, Amsterdam Ave. and W. 115th St., New York, N. Y.

COLBY, CHARLES WILLIAM, Ph. D., Professor McGill University, Montreal, Canada.

COLE, GEORGE C., Sheboygan, Wis.

*Cole, GEORGE WATSON, Riverside, Conn.

COLE, RUBLEE A., A. B., LL. B., Route No. 5, Station A., Milwaukee, Wis.

COLE, THEODORE LEE, Ph. B., 715 Colorado Bldg., Washington, D. C.

COLEMAN, CLARENCE, C. E., U. S. Assistant Engineer, Duluth, Minn.

COLEMAN, RT. REV. LEIGHTON, D. D., Wilmington, Del.

COLLES, MRS. JULIA KEESE, 20 High St., Morristown, N. J.

COLLIER, THEODORE, Ph. D., Williams College, Williamstown, Mass.

COLLINS, EDWARD DAY, Ph. D., Johnson, Vt.

COLLINS, MISS MARIA C., 1327 McMillan St., Walnut Hills, Cincinnati, Ohio.

COLLINS, V. LANSING, A. M., Princeton University, Princeton, N. J.

COLSTON, FREDERICK M., 216 E. Baltimore St., Baltimore, Md.

COLVILLE, EDITH C. (MRS. R. W.), 445 Monmouth Boulevard, Galesburg, Ill.

COLVIN, MISS CAROLINE, PH. D., Professor in University of Maine, Orono, Me.

CONAWAY, REV. HORACE MANN, A. M., Ph. D., D. D., Warren, Pa.

CONE, MRS. KATE MORRIS, Ph. D., Hartford, Vermont.

CONEY, JOHN HOUGHTON, A. M., Professor Princeton University, Princeton, N. J.

CONKLING, HON. ALFRED RONALD, Ph. B., LL. B., 76 William St., New York, N. Y.

CONNELLY, WILLIAM E., 621 Tyler St., Topeka, Kan.

CONNER, FRANCES S., High School, 919 Delaware St., Scranton, Pa.

CONNER, PRESTON M., 447 North 42nd St., West Philadelphia, Pa.

CONNER, PHILLIP SYNG PHYSICK, Rowlandsville, Md.

CONRAD, PROF. CLARENCE C., Belmont County Teachers' Institute, Bridgeport, Ohio.

CONRAD, HENRY C., 1009½ Market St., Wilmington, Del.

*CONSTANT, S. VICTOR, 120 Broadway, New York, N. Y.

CONWAY, MISS ESTELLE, B. A., Barron, Wis.

COOK, WEBSTER, Ph. D., Principal Saginaw East Side High School, Saginaw, Mich.

COOKE, GEORGE WILLIS, Wakefield Park, Wakefield, Mass.

COOKE, ROBERT GRIER, 507 5th Ave., New York, N. Y.

*COOLIDGE, ARCHIBALD CARY, Ph. D., Professor Harvard University, Randolph Hall, Cambridge, Mass.

*COOLIDGE, THOMAS JEFFERSON, JR., A. B., Old Colony Trust Company, Boston, Mass.

COOPER, MISS BESSIE DEAN, Rhode Island College, Kingston, R. I.

COOPER, HOMER H., A. M., Spiceland, Ind.

COPELAND, GEORGE E., 257 Lyon St., Milwaukee, Wis.

CORBERT, MISS ANITA LAWRENCE, Palo Alto, Cal. (Pacific Coast Branch.)

COREY, DELORAINE PENDRE, President Malden Historical Society, 2 Berkeley St., Malden, Mass.

COREY, ISABELLA HOLDEN (MRS. D. P.), 2 Berkeley St., Malden, Mass.

CORNING, HON. CHARLES ROBERT, A. M., Corresponding Secretary New Hampshire Historical Society, 52 Pleasant St., Concord, N. H.

CORTHELL, WILLIAM IRVING, A. B., 39 Walnut Park, Roxbury, Mass.

CORWIN, EDWARD SAMUEL, Ph. D., 10 Nassau, Princeton, N. J.

CORWIN, EDWARD TANJORE, D. D., New Brunswick, N. J.

COULTER, MISS ELVA C., A. B., 2 Westminster Terrace, Brighton, Mass.

COUPER, WALTER F., B. A., 307 Fifth Ave., S. E., Minneapolis, Minn.

COUSAR, MRS. ROBERT MOORE, 1760 Q St., Washington, D. C.

COUTANT, DR. RICHARD B., President of Historical Society of Tarrytown, Tarrytown, N. Y.

COWAN, ROBERT E., 867 Treat Ave., San Francisco, Cal. (Pacific Coast Branch.)

COWLES, ISRAEL TOWNE, Detroit, Mich.

COWLES, JOHN GUITEAU WELCH, A. M., LL. D., Cleveland, Ohio.

COX, EXUM MORRIS, Santa Rosa, Cal. (Pacific Coast Branch.)

COX, ISAAC JOSLIN, Ph. D., care of University of Cincinnati, Cincinnati, Ohio.

COX, JESSIE V., Aberdeen, South Dakota.

COX, JOSEPHINE M., 12, The Wyandot, Indianapolis, Ind.

COX, MISS MARY B., 88 Lafontaine St., Huntington, Ind.

COYNE, JAMES HENRY, M. A., St. Thomas, Ontario, Canada.

CRANDALL, BENJAMIN RAY, S. B., B. Ped., M. A., Superintendent of Schools, Rawlins, Wyo.

CRANDALL, FRANCIS ASBURY, 1636 16th St., N. W., Washington, D. C.

CRANDALL, SAMUEL BENJAMIN, S. B., Ph. D., 1831 F. St., N. W., Washington, D. C.

CRANE, HON. FREDERICK E., County Court Chambers, Kings County, Brooklyn, N. Y.

CRAPO, HON. WILLIAM W., LL. D., New Bedford, Mass.

CRAVEN, ISABEL (MRS. THOMAS L), Cravenhurst, Salem, N. J.

CRAWFORD, MRS. CLARENCE C., 500 Turner Ave., Columbia, Mo.

CRAWFORD, EUGENE L., P. O. Box 443, Union Springs, Ala.

CRAWFORD, WILLIAM HENRY, A. B., A. M., B. D., LL. D., D. D., President Allegheny College, Meadville, Pa.

CRISSMAN, GEORGE R., A. B., Superintendent Salina Public Schools, Salina, Kan.

CROCKER, MISS ANNETTE L., A. B., care St. Paul's School, Concord, N. H.

CROCKER, HENRY GRAHAM, M. L., 17 Iowa Circle, Washington, D. C.

CROFTON, FRANCIS BLAKE, A. B., Provincial Librarian of Nova Scotia, Halifax, N. S.

CRONKHITE, ELISHA PACKER, 115 Worth St., New York.

CROSS, ARTHUR LYON, Ph. D., University of Michigan, Ann Arbor, Mich.

CROTHERS, GEORGE EDWARD, A. M., 433 Mills Bldg., San Francisco, Cal. (Pacific Coast Branch.)

CROUCH, FLORA A., 136 N. Central Ave., Austin Station, Chicago, Ill.

CROWTHER, MISS ELIZABETH, A. M., 262 Glen St., Glens Falls, N. Y.; Instructor in History at Mt. Holyoke College, South Hadley, Mass.

CRUIKSHANK, LIEUT.-COL. ERNEST, Niagara Falls, Ontario, Canada.

CRUNDEN, FREDERICK MORGAN, A. M., Librarian Public Library, St. Louis, Mo.

CUNNINGHAM, HENRY C., Savannah, Ga.

CUNNINGHAM, HENRY W., A. B., 58 Fiske Building, 89 State St., Boston, Mass.

CURE, B. F., Jermyn, Pa.

CURREY, J. SEYMOUR, 1308 Judson Ave., Evanston, Ill.

CURRIE, CAMERON, Detroit, Mich.

CURRIER, CHARLES FRANCIS ADAMS, A. M., Professor Massachusetts Institute of Technology, Boston, Mass.

CURRIER, MRS. CLARA MAY, Proctor Academy, Andover, N. H.

CURTIS, GEORGE MUNSON, Meriden, Conn.

CURTIS, HON. WILLIAM ELEROY, A. B., A. M., Litt. D., Home Life Building, Washington, D. C.

CURTISS, CHARLES CHAUNCEY, Director Fine Arts Building, 203 Michigan Boulevard, Chicago, Ill.

CUSHING, FRANCIS J., 1013 Chamber of Commerce Bldg., Chicago, Ill.

CUSHING, HARRY ALONZO, LL. B., Ph. D., 43 Cedar St., New York, N. Y.

CUSHING, WALTER HOWARD, A. M., Principal High School, Framingham, Mass.

CUTLER, MISS MARY HELON, B. A., 32 Fern St., Auburndale, Mass.

CUTTER, LEONARD FRANCIS, A. M., 138 Harvard St., Brookline, Mass.

*DABNEY, RICHARD HEATH, M. A., Ph. D., Professor University of Virginia, Charlottesville, Va.

DAISH, JOHN BROUGHTON, A. B., LL. M., Kellogg Bldg., Washington, D. C.

DALLAS, MISS RHEA, Rockhill, S. C.

DALY, MISS KATHRYN HELEN, 2721 Channing Way, Berkeley, Cal. (Pacific Coast Branch.)

D'ANCONA, EDWARD N., 108 La Salle St., Chicago, Ill.

DANIEL, J. W. W., Wesleyan Female College, Macon, Ga.

DARMSTAEDTER, DR. PAUL, Ph. D., Wiesbadener-Strasse 22, Friedenau bie Berlin, Germany.

DAVENPORT, BENNETT F., M. D., President Historical Society of Watertown, 67 Coolidge Hill Road, Watertown, Mass.

DAVENPORT, MISS FRANCES GARDINER, Ph. D., Carnegie Institution, Washington, D. C.

DAVENPORT, HENRY B., 375 Pearl St., Brooklyn, N. Y.

DAVENPORT PUBLIC LIBRARY, Davenport, Iowa.

DAVIDSON, JOHN NELSON, A. M., Pastor Congregational Church, Dartford, Wis.

DAVIDSON, OTTO C., Iron Mountain, Mich.

DAVIS, ALICE, A. M., Teacher in Wadleigh High School, Whittier Hall, 1230 Amsterdam Ave., New York City.

*DAVIS, ANDREW MCFARLAND, A. M., 10 Appleton St., Cambridge, Mass.

DAVIS, 'ARTHUR KYLE, A. M., President Southern Female College, Petersburg, Va.

DAVIS, MISS BERTHA TAPPAN, 25 Sherman St., Springfield, Mass.

DAVIS, HON. DARNELL, C. M. G., Auditor General, Georgetown, British Guiana.

DAVIS, EDWARD HATTON, B. S., 126 South Grant St., West Lafayette, Ind.

DAVIS, GEORGE PERRIN, A. B., A. M., LL. B., President McLean County Historical Society, Bloomington, Ill.

DAVIS, H. JACKSON, A. B., Box 119, Marion, Va.

*DAVIS, HORACE, LL. D., 1800 Broadway, San Francisco, Cal. (Pacific Coast Branch.)

DAVIS, MISS JENNIE MELVENE, Hotel St. George, Brooklyn, N. Y.

DAVIS, JESSE B., Detroit Central High School, 186 Marston Ave., Detroit, Mich.

*DAVIS, HON. JOHN CHANDLER BANCROFT, LL. D., 1621 H St., Washington, D. C.

DAVIS, MADISON, 316 A St., S. E., Washington, D. C.

DAVIS, WALTER SCOTT, A. M., Secretary Wayne County, Indiana, Historical Society, High School, Richmond, Ind.

DAVIS, WARREN J., Marinette, Wis.

DAVIS, WILLIAM WATSON, Hartley Hall, Columbia University, New York, N. Y.

DAWKINS, WALTER I., 408-409 Fidelity Building, Baltimore, Md.

DAWSON, EDGAR, Princeton University, Princeton, N. J.

DAY, CLIVE, Ph. D., Professor Yale University, New Haven, Conn.

DEALEY, JAMES QUAYLE, Ph. D., Professor Brown University, Providence, R. I.

DEAN, BAILEY SUTTON, Professor of History, Hiram College, Hiram, Ohio.

DEAN, CLARA B., B. A., M. A., 151 W. 70th St., New York, N. Y.

DEAN, HON. HENRY STEWART, Ann Arbor, Mich.

DEAN, MISS SARAH MARIA, A. B., 362 Commonwealth Ave., Boston, Mass.

DEANE, FANNIE B., State Normal School, Salem, Mass.

*DEATS, HIRAM EDMUND, Librarian Hunterdon County Historical Society, Flemington, N. J.

*DEFOREST, MAURICE ARNOLD, 2 Rue de l'Elysee, Paris, France.

DENHAM, EDWARD, New Bedford, Mass.

DENNIS, ALFRED LEWIS PINNEO, Ph. D., Professor of European History, University of Wisconsin. Madison, Wis.

DENNIS, ALFRED PEARCE, Ph. D., Professor Smith College, Northampton, Mass.

DENT, THOMAS, 65 Portland Block, 107 Dearborn St., Chicago, Ill.

DE PEYSTER, GEN. JOHN WATTS, A. M., Litt. D., Ph. D., LL. D., Rose Hill, Tivoli, New York.

DERBY, SAMUEL CARROLL, A. M., Professor Ohio State University, Columbus, Ohio.

DE RENNE, W. J., Westport Inn, Westport, N. Y.

DESMOND, HUMPHREY J., 846 Wells Building, Milwaukee, Wis.

DETROIT PUBLIC LIBRARY, Detroit, Mich.

DEVITT, REV. PROF. EDWARD IGNATIUS, S. J., Georgetown University, Washington, D. C.

DEVOL, RUSSELL S., A. M., Kenyon College, Gambier, Ohio.

DEWEL, WILLIAM C., Clerk of District Court, Algona, Iowa.

DeWITT, F. M., 364 Sutter St., San Francisco, Cal. (Pacific Coast Branch.)

DE WITT, JOHN, D. D., LL. D., Professor of Church History, Theological Seminary, Princeton, N. J.

*DEXTER, FRANKLIN BOWDITCH, A. M., Litt. D., Assistant Librarian, Professor Yale University, New Haven, Conn.

DE YO, LOU IRENE, Red Bluff, Cal.

DE ZAVALA, MISS ADINA, 117 4th St., San Antonio, Texas.

DICKINSON, ALBERT, West Taylor St. and The River, Chicago, Ill.

DICKINSON, HON. DON M., Detroit, Mich.

DICKSON, G. A., Principal of High School, Newcastle, Pa.

DIELMAN, LOUIS HENRY, A. M., 1401 John St., Baltimore, Md.

DIETZ, WILLIAM G., Citizens Building, 57 Cutler St., Cleveland, Ohio.

DIFFENDEIFFER, FRANK RIED, Litt. D., Lancaster, Pa.

DIGGLES, MISS GRACE P., Millbrae, Cal.

DILLON, AUGUSTUS REYNOLDS, 524 West 64th St., Chicago, Ill.

DILWORTH, JAMES FRANCIS, 28 Lincoln St., Jersey City, N. J.

DIMOCK, MRS. HENRY FARNAM, 25 E. 60th St. New York.

DIMOCK, MISS MARY J., 907 N. Broad St., Elizabeth, N. J.

DINKINS, JAMES, 2025 Coliseum, New Orleans, La.

DINSMORE, SUSAN B., Eugene, Ore. (Pacific Coast Branch.)

DODD, MISS LENA, Kalama, Wash. (Pacific Coast Branch.)

DODD, WALTER FAIRLEIGH, Library of Congress, 210 A St., S. E. Washington, D. C.

DODD, WILLIAM EDWARD, Ph. D., Professor Randolph-Macon College, Ashland, Va.

DODGE, ROBERT G., Assistant Attorney General of Commonwealth of Massachusetts, 60 State St., Boston, Mass.

DODGE, THEODORE AYRAULT, LL. B., Colonel U. S. A., 42 Broadway, New York, N. Y.

DOGGETT, SAMUEL BRADLEE, Commonwealth Ave. and Wade St., Boston, Mass.

DOOLITTLE, WILLIAM SHEARMAN, A. B., Utica, N. Y.

DORR, HARVEY EMMONDS, 629 Elm St., College Park, Cal. (Pacific Coast Branch.)

DORSEY, J. S., Columbia, Mo.

DOUGHERTY, REV. M. ANGELO, A. M., 77 Lake View Ave., Cambridge, Mass.

DOUGLAS, CHARLES H., 120 Boylston St., Boston, Mass.

DOUGLAS, SAMUEL TOWNSEND, 2d, Ph. D., Detroit, Mich.

DOUGLAS, WALTER B., A. B., LL. B., Judge of Circuit Court of 8th Judicial Circuit of Missouri, St. Louis, Mo.

DOUGLASS, GAYLORD W., A. B., Boys' Industrial School, San Jose, Cal.

DOUSMAN, MRS. NINA STURGIS, Prairie du Chien, Wis.

DOW, EARLE WILBUR, A. B., University of Michigan, Ann Arbor, Mich.

DOW, GEORGE FRANCIS, Secretary Essex Institute, Salem, Mass.

DRINKARD, ALFRED W., M. S., Virginia Polytechnic Institute, Blacksburg, Va.

DRUMMOND, WILLIAM HENRY, M. D., 2482 St. Catherine St., Montreal, Canada.

DRURY, JOHN BENJAMIN, D. D., P. O. Box 2117, New York, N. Y.

DU BOSE, JOEL C., A. M., University, Ala.

DUDLEY, CHARLES BENJAMIN, Ph. D., Drawer 156, Altoona, Pa.

DU FOUR, CLARENCE J., 689 Shepard Ave., Milwaukee, Wis. (Pacific Coast Branch.)

DULLES, CHARLES WINSLOW, M. D., Lecturer on History of Medicine, University of Pennsylvania, 4101 Walnut St., Philadelphia, Pa.

DULLES, JOSEPH HEATLY, A. M., Librarian Theological Seminary, Princeton, N. J.

DUNCAN, DAVID S., University of Denver, University Park, Colo.

DUNCAN, GEORGE WEBSTER, M. S., Auburn, Ala.

DUNCAN, MURRAY MORRIS, E. M., Ishpeming, Mich.

DUNIWAY, CYLDE AUGUSTUS, Ph. D., Professor Stanford University, Cal. (Pacific Coast Branch.)

DUNN, CLARA BELLE, 7093 12th St., Ann Arbor, Mich.

DUNNING, WILLIAM ARCHIBALD, Ph. D., LL. D., Professor Columbia University, New York.

DURAND, JOHN STEWART, LL. B., 81 Fulton St., New York, N. Y.

DURAND, LOYAL, B. L., LL. B., Milwaukee, Wis.

DURFEE, EDWARD LEWIS, A. B., 95 Cottage St., New Haven, Conn.

DURRETT, REUBEN THOMAS, LL.D., Louisville, Ky.

DUTCHER, GEORGE MATTHEW, Ph. D., Professor of History, Wesleyan University, Middletown, Conn.

DURSTINE, WARREN, 310 Nicholson St., Joliet, Ill.

DUTTERA, REV. WILLIAM B., B. D., Ph. D., Salisbury, N. C.

DUTTON, SAMUEL T., A. M., Professor in Teacher's College, Columbia University, New York, N. Y.

DWYER, JEREMIAH, Detroit, Mich.

DYER, ALBION M., 2250 Euclid Ave., Cleveland, Ohio.

DYER, MISS LAURA E., High School, San Diego, Cal. (Pacific Coast Branch.)

DYNES, SARAH A., State Normal School, Trenton, N. J.

EARLHAM HISTORICAL CLUB, Richmond, Ind.

EATON, HON. AMASA M., A. M., LL. B., Providence, R. I.

EAVES, MISS LUCILE, A. B., 515 West 111th St., New York, N. Y. (Pacific Coast Branch.)

EBERHARDT, HON. MAX, LL. M., D. C. L., 436 Ashland Boulevard, Chicago, Ill.

EBERT, ALBERT E., M. D., Ph. D., 426 State St., Chicago, Ill.

ECHOLS, SILAS, Mt. Vernon Township High School, 612 East Broadway, Mt. Vernon, Ill.

ECKARD, REV. LEIGHTON WILSON, D. D., 103 N. 4th St., Easton, Pa.

ECKELS, HON. JAMES HERRON, A. M., Chicago, Ill.

ECKENRODE, HAMILTON JAMES, 1513 John St., Baltimore, Md.

ECKHARDT, CARL CONRAD, Ph. B., M. A., Barns Hall, Cornell University, Ithaca, N. Y.

*EDES, HENRY HERBERT, A. M., Treasurer of The Colonial Society of Massachusetts, 28 State St., Boston, Mass.

EDGERTON, MISS MYRA T., Teacher of History, Jamaica High School, Jamaica, N. Y.

EDMONDS, FRANKLIN SPENCER, A. M., Ph. B., LL. B., Honorary Lecturer in Political Science, Central High School, Philadelphia, Pa.; Asst. Professor of Law, Swarthmore College, Swarthmore, Pa.

EDMONDS, RICHARD H., Manufacturers' Record, Baltimore, Md.

EDWARDS, JOSEPH PLIMSOLL, Londonderry, Nova Scotia.

EDWARDS, MISS MARTHA L., 6 Linton St., Cincinnati, Ohio.

EGAN. JOHN M., Kansas City Terminal Railway Co., 22d and Grand Ave., Kansas City, Mo.

EGGLESTON, GEORGE CARY, 188 W. 135th St., New York, N. Y.

EGLESTON, MELVILLE, A. M., 18 Cortlandt St., New York, N. Y.

EHRICH, LOUIS R., Manhattan Square Hotel, 50 W. 77th St., New York, N. Y.

ELDREDGE, ARCH BISHOP, A. B., Marquette, Mich.

ELDREDGE, ZOETH S., 2621 Devisadero St., San Francisco, Cal. (Pacific Coast Branch.)

ELDRIDGE, MISS ISABELLA, Norfolk, Conn.

ELLERY, MISS ELOISE, Ph. D., Vassar College, Poughkeepsie, N. Y.

ELLIOT, CHARLES DARWIN, Somerville, Mass.

ELLIOT, FRANK M., Room 600, 123 La Salle St., Chicago, Ill.

ELLIOTT, MISS AGNES, State Normal School, Los Angeles, Cal. (Pacific Coast Branch.)

ELLIOTT, EDWARD G., Ph. D., Princeton, N. J.

ELLIOTT, MISS LUCY ELVIRA, A. B., Troy, Mich.

ELLIOTT, THOMPSON C., A. B., 314 East Poplar St., Walla Walla, Wash. (Pacific Coast Branch.)

ELLIS, EDWARD S., A. M., 39 N. Fullerton Ave., Montclair, N. J.

ELLIS, MISS ELLEN DEBORAH, Ph. D., Instructor in History, Mount Holyoke College, South Hadley, Mass.

ELLIS, HENRY A., Village Superintendent, Colton, Wash.

ELLSWORTH, REV. WOLCOTT WEBSTER, B. A., 301 South William St., Johnstown, N. Y.

ELSBERG, ALBERT M., 73 East 66th St., New York, N. Y.

ELSON, HENRY W., Ph. D., Litt. D., Ohio University, Athens, Ohio.

ELTING, IRVING, LL. B., 54 Market St., Poughkeepsie, N. Y.

ELY, THEODORE NEWEL, C. E., A. M., Sc. D., Broad Street Station, Philadelphia, Pa.

ELZAS, BARNETT A., M. D., LL. D., Rabbi of Beth Elohim Synagogue, Charleston, S. C.

EMERSON, SAMUEL FRANKLIN, Ph. D., Burlington, Vermont.

EMERTON, EPHRAIM, Ph. D., Professor Harvard University, Cambridge, Mass.

ENDICOTT, WILLIAM CROWNINSHIELD, A. B., Danvers Centre, Mass.

ENELOW, RABBI H. G., D. D., 1115 Hepburn Ave., Louisville, Ky.

ENGLISH, HENRY FOWLER, LL. B., 38 Hillhouse Ave., New Haven, Conn.

ENOCH PRATT FREE LIBRARY, Baltimore, Md.

ENSIGN, CHARLES SIDNEY, LL. B., Billings Park, Newton, Mass.

EPPSTEIN, MRS. EMILY KEITH, B. L., M. L., Cebu, P. I.

ESBERG, A. I., 2211 Pacific Ave., San Francisco, Cal. (Pacific Coast Branch.)

ESSEX INSTITUTE, Salem, Mass.

EVANS, MRS. ALLEN B., 883 Fulton St., San Francisco, Cal. (Pacific Coast Branch.)

EVANS, EDWARD S., Virginia State Library, 509 E. Franklin St., Richmond, Va.

EVANS, MISS ELIZABETH G., B. A., 4126 Chester Ave., Philadelphia, Pa.

EVANS, LAWRENCE B., Ph. D., Professor of History Tufts College, Tufts College, Mass.

EVANS, HON. NELSON WILEY, A. M., LL. B., Portsmouth, Ohio.

EVANS, WILLIAM LINCOLN, B. L., LL. B., Green. Bay, Wis.

EVANSTON PUBLIC LIBRARY, Evanston, Ill.

EVERETT, WILLIAM ELLIS, Sycamore, Ill.

EVJEN, JOHN O., Ph. D., Gettysburg, Pa.

EWELL, JOHN LOUIS, D. D., 325 College St., Washington, D. C.

EWING, MAJ. E. W. R., A. M., LL. B., Washington, D. C.

EWING, JAMES REES, Ph. D., Station G, N. W., Washington, D. C.

EWING, JOHN GILLESPIE, A. M., 639 Fullerton Ave., Chicago, Ill.

*FAILING, HENRIETTA ELLESON, 5th and Taylor Sts., Portland, Ore. (Pacific Coast Branch.)

FAILING, JAMES F., 243 11th St., Portland, Ore. (Pacific Coast Branch.)

*FAILING, MARY FORBUSH, 5th and Taylor Sts., Portland, Ore. (Pacific Coast Branch.)

FAIR, EUGENE, A. B., 809 East Harrison St., Kirksville, Mo.

FAIRBANKS, MISS ELSIE DANIELS, B. A., 527 Hanover St., Manchester, N. H.

FAIRBANKS, MISS MAY LAVINIA, Ph. D., Librarian Cornell College, Mount Vernon, Iowa.

FAIRLEY, WILLIAM, Ph. D., 1210 Bedford Ave., Brooklyn, N. Y.

FANNING, HON. A. C., Towanda, Pa.

FARNAM, HENRY WALCOTT, M. A., R. P. D., 43 Hillhouse Ave., New Haven, Conn.

FARNHAM, AMOS W., Teacher of Geography in Oswego State Normal and Training School, Oswego, N. Y.

FARNHAM, MISS MARY FRANCES, Dean of Women, Pacific University, Forest Grove, Ore. (Pacific Coast Branch.)

FARRAND, MAX, Ph. D., Professor of History, Stanford University, Cal. (Pacific Coast Branch.)

FAULKNER, JOHN ALFRED, Professor Theological Seminary, Madison, N. J.

FAY, CHARLES RALPH, B. A., M. A., 135 Remsen St., Brooklyn, N. Y.

FAY, SIDNEY BRADSHAW, Ph. D., Professor Dartmouth College, Hanover N. H.

FELCH, THEODORE ALPHEUS, Ph. B., M. D., Ishpeming, Mich.

FELLOWS, GEORGE EMORY, Ph. D., L. H. D., LL. D., President of University of Maine, Orono, Me.

FENN, PROF. WILLIAM WALLACE, A. M., S. T. B., 176 Upland Road, Cambridge, Mass.

FENTON, WILLIAM DAVID, 609-14 Fenton Building, Portland, Ore. (Pacific Coast Branch.)

FERGUS, GEORGE H., 22 Lake St., Chicago, Ill.

FERGUSON, HENRY, A. M., LL. D., Professor Trinity College, Hartford, Conn.

FERGUSON, WILLIAM SCOTT, Ph. D., Professor University of California, Berkeley, Cal. (Pacific Coast Branch.)

FERRIS, ALFRED J., 3409 Baring St., Philadelphia, Pa.

FERRIS, ANNETTE E. K., A. M., Principal High School, Trinidad, Col.

FERRIS, MISS ELEANOR, A. M., 2016 Scottwood Ave., Toledo, Ohio.

FERRY, CHARLES H., 183 Lincoln Park Boulevard, Chicago, Ill.

FERRY, HON. DEXTER MASON, Detroit, Mich.

FERTIG, JAMES WALTER, Ph. D., Lewis Institute, Chicago, Ill.

FESLER, MAYO, Secretary, The Civic Improvement League of St. Louis, 3957 McPherson Ave., St. Louis, Mo.

FICKLEN, JOHN ROSE, B. Let., Professor Tulane University, New Orleans, La.

FIELD, FRED F., Attorney at Law, State House, Boston, Mass.

FILES, GEORGE TAYLOR, Ph. D., Professor Bowdoin College, Brunswick, Maine.

FINLEY, JOHN H., Ph. D., LL. D., President College of City of New York, New York, N. Y.

FINNEY, BYRON ALFRED, A. B., University of Michigan Library, Ann Arbor, Mich.

FIRTH, MISS MARTHA, Pella, Iowa.

FISH, CARL RUSSELL, A. B., A. M., Ph. D., Assistant Professor of American History, University of Wisconsin, 248 Langdon St., Madison, Wis.

FISH, MARY E., Greenville, Mich.

FISHER, MISS ANNA ANDERSON, High School, Cedar Rapids, Iowa.

FISHER, HENRY BENEDICT, A. B., Superintendent of Public Schools, Geneseo, Ill.

FISHER, RAY D., Ph. D., Assistant Professor of History and Economics, Willamette University, Salem, Ore. (Pacific Coast Branch.)

FISHER, RICHARD D., 1420 Park Ave., Baltimore, Md.

FISHER, SYDNEY GEORGE, L. H. D., LL. D., 328 Chestnut St., Philadelphia, Pa.

FISHER, WILLARD CLARK, Professor Wesleyan University, Middletown, Conn.

FISK, REV. CHARLES EZRA, Ph. D., Viola, Ill.

FITCH, HON. FERRIS SMITH, A. B., Tucson, Ariz.

FITE, EMERSON DAVID, Instructor in History, Yale University, 90 Avon St., New Haven, Conn.

FITZPATRICK, JOHN C., Library of Congress, Washington, D. C.

FLAGG, CHARLES ALLCOTT, A. B., B. L. S., M. A., Catalogue Division, Library of Congress, Washington, D. C.

FLAGG, MISS LOUISE E., Wheaton Seminary, Norton, Mass.

FLEMING, WALTER L., A. M., Ph. D., Professor of History, West Virginia University, Morgantown, W. Va.

FLEXNER, MISS MARY, 417 West 118th St., New York, N. Y.

FLICK, ALEXANDER CLARENCE, Ph. D., Litt. D., Professor of European History, Syracuse University, Syracuse, N. Y.

FLICK, DR. LAWRENCE F., 736 Pine St., Philadelphia, Pa.

FLICKINGER, HON. J. R., A. M., Principal State Normal School, Lock Haven, Pa.

FLING, FRED MORROW, Ph. D., Professor University of Nebraska, Lincoln, Neb.

FLINT, WESTON BROWN, A. B., A. M., 55 Trowbridge St., Cambridge, Mass.

FLISCH, MISS JULIA A., M. A., 424 Murray St., Madison, Wis.

FOGARTY, JOSEPH N., M. D., Key West, Fla.

FOOTE, MISS ANNA E., Ph. B., Dept. of History in Normal School, Jamaica, N. Y.

FOOTE, ARTHUR DE WINT, Grass Valley, Cal. (Pacific Coast Branch.)

FORD, GUY STANTON, B. L., Ph. D., 1010½ West California St., Urbana, Ill.

FORD, HENRY JONES, *Pittsburg Gazette*, Pittsburg, Pa.

FORD, THOMAS BENJAMIN, 101 Bridge St., Trenton, Mo.

FORD, WORTHINGTON CHAUNCEY, Chief of Division of Manuscripts, Library of Congress, Washington, D. C.

FOREMAN, C. J., Harbor Springs, Mich.

FORREST, ELIZABETH, 3264 Groveland Ave., Chicago, Ill.

FORGAN, DAVID ROBERTSON, Vice-President First National Bank, Chicago, Ill.

FORGAN, JAMES BERWICK, President First National Bank, Chicago, Ill.

FORMAN, SAMUEL E., The Plymouth, Washington, D. C.

FORTIER, ALCEE, D. Litt., Professor Tulane University, New Orleans, La.

Foss, Claude W., Ph. D., Professor Augustana College, Rock Island, Illinois.

Foster, Francis Apthorp, 24 Milk St., Boston, Mass.

Foster, Frederick Coffin, A. M., Professor St. Lawrence University, Canton, N. Y.

Foster, Herbert Darling, A. M., Professor Dartmouth College, Hanover, N. H.

Foster, John W., 1323 18th St., Washington, D. C.

Foster, Roger, A. M., 35 Wall St., New York, N. Y.

*Foster, William Eaton, A. M., Litt. D., Librarian Public Library, Providence, R. I.

Foulke, Hon. William Dudley, A. M., Richmond, Ind.

Fowler, John, 719 Chestnut St., St. Louis, Mo.

Fox, George Levi, LL. B., A. M., The University School, New Haven, Conn.

Fox, John Sharpless, University High School, Chicago, Ill.

Fox, Right Rev. J. J., D. D., Bishop of Green Bay, Green Bay, Wis.

Fox, Miss Stella Robinson, A. B., Wilson College, Chambersburg, Pa.

Fradenburgh, Adelbert Grant, Ph. D., Professor Adelphi College, Brooklyn, N. Y.

Franklin, Frank George, Ph. D., Professor of History and Political Science, University of the Pacific, San Jose, Cal. (Pacific Coast Branch.)

Francisco, Louis Joseph, Richmond, Ind.

Fraser, Alexander Hugh Ross, LL. B., Librarian Cornell University, Boardman Hall, Ithaca, N. Y.

Frazer, Hon. Allan Howard, Ph. B., Detroit, Mich.

Freeman, Archibald, A. M., Andover, Mass.

Freeman, Hiram Guernsey, Appleton, Wis.

Freeman, Ralph, B. A., 351 Adelphi St., Brooklyn, N. Y.

Freer, Charles Lang, M. A., Detroit, Mich.

French, Harry Banks, 429 Arch St., Philadelphia, Pa.

French, Mary L., Pomona, Cal. (Pacific Coast Branch.)

Friedenwald, Herbert, Ph. D., 356 Second Ave., New York, N. Y.

Friendly, S. M., Eugene, Ore. (Pacific Coast Branch.)

Friends Free Library, Germantown, Philadelphia, Pa.

Fries, Miss Adelaide L., 224 Cherry St., Winston-Salem, N. C.

Frost, George Frederick, A. M., 303 Benefit St., Providence, R. I.

Frost, Miss Lilla, Harvard, Mass.

Fry, Charles, 21 Commonwealth Ave., Boston, Mass.

Fryer, Charles Edmund, A. M., The New Sherbrook, Montreal, Canada.

Fuller, Louise Stetson, 150 Elm St., Northampton, Mass.

FULLER, MARY BREESE, Fredonia, N. Y.

FULLER, HON. MELVILLE WESTON, LL. D., Chief Justice of the United States, Washington, D. C.

FULLER, PAUL F., 71 Broadway, New York.

FULLER, REV. SAMUEL RICHARD, care of Brown, Shipley & Co., 123 Pall Mall, S. W., London, England.

FULLER, WILLIAM A., 2913 Michigan Ave., Chicago, Ill.

FUNK, HENRY DANIEL, M. A., 29 Macalester Ave., St. Paul, Minn.

FURNESS, WILLIAM ELIOT, A. B., A. M., LL. B., 417 Orchard St., Chicago, Ill.

FURR, REV. WALTER ESPY, Greenville, Ky.

GAGE, HON. LYMAN J., LL. D., President United States Trust Co., New York City.

GAHAN, WILLIAM J., Plaquemine, La.

GAILOR, RT. REV. THOMAS FRANK, A. M., Bishop of Tennessee, Sewanee, Tenn.

GALBRAITH, THOMAS R., 1920 East Pacific St., Philadelphia, Pa.

GALLAHER, GEORGE P., 5046 Jefferson Ave., Chicago, Ill.

GALLAHER, MISS SARAH M., M. A., 404 West 124th St., New York, N. Y.

GALLAUDET, EDWARD MINER, Ph. D., LL. D., President Gallaudet College, Washington, D. C.

GALLINGER, HERBERT P., Ph. D., Dept. of History, Amherst College, Amherst, Mass.

GALLOWAY, FRANCES HANEY, Monmouth, Ore. (Pacific Coast Branch.)

GAMBRILL, J. MONTGOMERY, 2102 Chelsea Terrace, Baltimore, Md.

GARDINER, FREDERIC, A. M., The Yeates School, Lancaster, Pa.

GARDNER, ADDISON L., 1020 Royal Insurance Bldg., Chicago, Ill.

GARDNER, HENRY BRAYTON, Ph. D., Professor Brown University, 54 Stimson Ave., Providence, R. I.

GARFIELD, HARRY AUGUSTUS, A. B., Dept. of Jurisprudence and Politics, Princeton University, Princeton, N. J.

GARFIELD, JAMES RUDOLPH, A. B., Secretary of the Interior, Washington, D. C.

GARNEAU, HECTOR, B. C. L., 320 Prince Arthur St., Montreal, Canada.

GARNETT, JAMES M., 1316 Bolton St., Baltimore, Md.

GARRARD, COL. JEPTHA, LL. B., 44 Johnston Building, Cincinnati, O.

GARRETT, ROBERT, A. B., B. Sc., Continental Building, Baltimore, Md.

GARRISON, GEORGE PIERCE, Ph. D., Professor University of Texas, Austin, Texas.

GARVER, FRANK HARMON, Morningside College, Sioux City, Iowa.

GASKILL, FRANCIS A., Superior Court, Court House, Boston, Mass.

GATES, MERRILL EDWARDS, Ph. D., LL. D., L. H. D., 1309 Rhode Island Ave., Washington, D. C.

GAY, EDWIN FRANCIS, Ph. D., 58 Highland St., Cambridge, Mass.

GAY, FRANK BUTLER, Librarian Watkinson Library of Reference, Hartford, Conn.

*GAY, H. NELSON, A. M., Palazzo Orsini, Rome, Italy.

GAY, MARTIN, B. S., C. E., 103 East 125th St., New York, N. Y.

GEER, CURTIS MANNING, Ph. D., Professor of Church History, Hartford Theological Seminary, Hartford, Conn.

GEISER, KARL FREDERICK, Ph. D., 915 Tremont St., Cedar Falls, Iowa.

GELSTRAP, W. G., Eugene, Ore. (Pacific Coast Branch.)

GEROULD, JAMES THAYER, A. B., University of Minnesota, Minneapolis, Minn.

GERRISH, MISS CLARIBEL, 13 Park St., Haverhill, Mass.

*GERRY, HON. ELBRIDGE THOMAS, A. M., 261 Broadway, New York.

GERSCHANEK, S., Principal Harlem Preparatory School, 2177 Eighth Ave., New York, N. Y.

GILBERT, HENRY KIDDER, 637 Railway Exchange, Chicago, Ill.

GILDAY, ANNA C., 1406 Wabash Ave., Kansas City, Mo.

*GILDER, RICHARD WATSON, L. H. D., LL. D., 33 E. 17th St., New York.

GILLETT, RUFUS WOODWARD, Detroit, Mich.

GILLIS, JAMES A., Salem, Mass.

GILLMORE, MARY B., 419 W. 118th St., New York, N. Y.

*GILMAN, ARTHUR, A. M., Cambridge, Mass.

*GILMAN, DANIEL COIT, LL. D., 614 Park Ave., Baltimore, Md.

GIROUS, REV. LOUIS, A. M., American International College, Springfield, Mass.

GLASCOCK, WILLIAM LEON, Box 663, Colton, Cal. (Pacific Coast Branch.)

GLASHAN, J. C., LL. D., School Inspector's Office, Ottawa, Canada.

GLENN, GARRARD, A. B., LL. B., 32 Nassau St., New York, N. Y.

GLESSNER, J. J., 1800 Prairie Ave., Chicago, Ill.

GLISON, RODNEY L., Chamber of Commerce Building, Portland, Ore. (Pacific Coast Branch.)

GODARD, GEORGE S., D. D., Librarian Connecticut State Library, Hartford, Conn.

GODDARD, WILLIAM, A. M., LL. D., 50 S. Main St., Providence, R. I.

GOEBEL, PROFESSOR JULIUS, Stanford University, Cal.

GOLDSMITH, MISS ADA, 816 Sutter St., San Francisco, Cal.

GOODRICH, FRANK, Ph. D., Professor Williams College, Williamstown, Mass.

GOODWIN, ELLIOT HERSEY, A. B., A. M., Ph. D., 79 Wall St., New York City.

GOODWIN, FRANK P., A. M., 3435 Observatory Road, Cincinnati, Ohio.

GORDON, ULYSSES G., Taylorville, Ill.

GORDY, WILBUR F., Superintendent of Schools, Springfield, Mass.

GORHAM, HON. GEORGE CONGDON, 1763 Q St., N. W., Washington, D. C.

GOSS, HON. ELBRIDGE HENRY, Melrose, Mass.

GOULD, ELGIN RALSTON LOVELL, Ph. D., 281 Fourth Ave., New York, N. Y.

GOULDER, HARVEY DANFORTH, Cleveland, Ohio.

GRAHAM, PROFESSOR ALEXANDER, Charlotte, N. C.

GRAHAM, MISS EMILY L., Cynwyd Road, Cynwyd, Pa.

GRANT, HON. CLAUDIUS BUCHANAN, LL. D., Justice Supreme Court of Michigan, Lansing, Mich.

GRANT, MISS MARY (for State Normal School Library), Winona, Minn.

GRATIOT, C. C., M. D., Shullsburg, Wis.

GRAVES, FRANK P., 734 First National Bank Bldg., Chicago, Ill.

GRAVES, HENRY CLINTON, A. M., D. D., 187 Elm St., West Somerville, Mass.

GRAY, JOHN HENRY, Ph. D., Professor Northwestern University, Evanston, Ill.

GRAY, MISS NELLIE, State Normal School, 630 High St., Bellingham, Wash.

GRAY, WILLIAM JOHN, A. B., Detroit, Mich.

GREELY, GEN. ADOLPHUS WASHINGTON, U. S. Army, Washington, D. C.

GREEN, HOWARD C., 419 West 118th St., New York, N. Y.

*GREEN, HON. SAMUEL ABBOTT, LL. D., Librarian and Vice-President Massachusetts Historical Society, 1154 Boylston St., Boston, Mass.

*GREEN, SAMUEL SWEET, A. M., Member of the Council of the American Antiquarian Society, Librarian Free Public Library, Worcester, Mass.

GREENE, EVARTS BOUTELL, Ph. D., Professor University of Illinois, Urbana, Ill.

GREENE, GEN. FRANCIS VINTON, U. S. A., Ellicott Square, Buffalo, N. Y.

*GREENE, JOHN, A. M., LL. B., Editor-in-Chief, Bradstreet's, New York, N. Y.

GREENE, LEWIS D., Captain U. S. Army, 244 E. 47th St., Chicago, Ill.

GREENE, MISS MARIA LOUISE, Ph. D., 14 University Place, New Haven, Conn.

GREENE, RICHARD HENRY, A. M., LL. B., 235 Central Park West, New York, N. Y.

GREENOUGH, CHESTER N., A. B., A. M., Ph. D., 20 Holworthy Hall, Cambridge, Mass.

GRIFFIN, MARTIN IGNATIUS JOSEPH, Editor of *The American Catholic Historical Researches*, Ridley Park, Pa.

*GRIFFIS, WILLIAM ELLIOT, D. D., L. H. D., President De Witt Historical Society of Tompkins County, Ithaca, N. Y.

GRISSOM, REV. WILLIAM LEE, Greensboro, N. C.

GRISWOLD, GEORGE C., Ph. D., Oregon Public Schools, Oregon, Ill.

GROGG, MARCELLUS SCOTT, Superintendent of Schools, Ridgeville, Ind.

GROSS, CHARLES, Ph. D., Professor Harvard University, Cambridge, Mass.

GROSVENOR, EDWIN AUGUSTUS, A. M., L.L D., Professor Amherst College, Amherst, Mass.

GROUARD, HANS ERNST, 5717 Madison Ave., Chicago, Ill.

GROUARD, MISS MARIA LOUISE, Marlborough School, Los Angeles, Cal.

GUERNSEY, MISS JESSIE E., 112 Lake St., New Britain, Conn.

GUERNSEY, ROCELLUS SHERIDAN, 58 Pine St., New York, N. Y.

GUINN, JAMES MILLER, A. M., Secretary Historical Society of Southern California, 5539 Monte Vista St., Los Angeles, Cal.

GUITTARD, FRANCIS GEVRIER, Associate Professor of History and Economics, Baylor University, Waco, Texas.

GUNTHER, CHARLES F., 212 State St., Chicago, Ill.

GWYNNE, MISS OLIVE MAY, 9th Ave. and 11th St., Lewiston, Idaho.

HADLEY, ARTHUR TWINING, LL. D., President Yale University, New Haven, Conn.

HADLEY, MISS SARAH L., A. M., 49 Dana St., Cambridge, Mass.

HAESELER, LOUISE H., Philadelphia High School for Girls, 2009 Mt. Vernon St., Philadelphia, Pa.

HAGERMAN, JAMES, JR., LL. B., 606 Wainwright Blld., St. Louis, Mo.

*HAGERMAN, JAMES J., Colorado Springs, Col.

HAGNER, HON. ALEXANDER BURTON, LL. D., Vice-President Columbia Historical Society, 1818 H St., Washington, D. C.

HAIGHT, THERON WILBER, Waukesha, Wis.

HAINES, MISS JANE BOWNE, A. M., Cheltenham, Pa.

HAIRE, HON. NORMAN WASHINGTON, LL. B., A. B., Houghton, Mich.

HALDERMAN, GEN. JOHN A., LL. D., Metropolitan Club, Washington, D. C.

HALL, MISS EDITH ROCKWELL, A. B., Balliol School, Utica, N. Y.

HALL, FRANK LORENZO, A. B., 30 Broad St., New York, N. Y.

HALL, JOHN OTIS, JR., A. B., Principal High School, Millbury, Mass.

HALL, JUSTUS OTHO, A. B., Superintendent of Schools, Beloit, Kan.

HALL, LYMAN BRONSON, A. B., B. D., 209 W. College St., Oberlin, Ohio.

HALLEY, ROBERT AMBROSE, M. D., 455 Old Colony Building, Chicago, Ill.

*HALL, HON. THEODORE PARSONS, A. M., Detroit, Mich.

HALLOWELL, MISS HENRIETTA TRACY, Milton, Mass.

HALPIN, ROBERT JOHN, A. B., A. M., Brunswick School, Greenwich, Conn.

HALSEY, MISS CORA MOORE, 1515 Marshall St., Manitowoc, Wis.

HALSEY, FRANCIS W., 7 West 43rd St., New York, N. Y.

HALSEY, JOHN JULIUS, LL. D., Lake Forest, Ill.

HAMERSLEY, WILLIAM, LL. D., Associate Judge of the Supreme Court of Errors, Hartford, Conn.

HAMILTON, JOSEPH GREGOIRE DE ROULHAC, M. A., Hillsboro, N. C.

HAMILTON, JOHN GAILLARD, A. B., Mobile, Ala.

HAMILTON, HON. PETER JOSEPH, A. M., Mobile, Ala.

HAMLIN, HON. CHARLES SUMNER, A. M., LL. D., 2 Raleigh St., Boston, Mass.

HAMLIN, FRANK, 107 Dearborn St., Chicago, Ill.

HAMLIN, TEUNIS SLINGERLAND, D. D., Vice-President Memorial Association of District of Columbia, 1306 Connecticut Ave., Washington, D. C.

HAMMER, ROSAMOND SWAN (Mrs. A. E.), Branford, Conn.

HAMMOND, NELLIE, Woburn, Mass.

HANCE, JOHN A., 311 West 106th St., New York, N. Y.

HANEY, JOHN LOUIS, Ph. D., Professor of English and History, Central High School, Philadelphia, Pa.

HANNA, MRS. MARCUS ALONZO, Cleveland, Ohio.

HANSEN, HERBERT C., 417 N. Hoyne Ave., Chicago, Ill.

HAPPER, EMILY FOSTER (MRS. F. A.), Librarian Public Library, Mobile, Ala.

HARBOLD, PETER MONROE, Ph. B., A. M., First Pennsylvania State Normal School, Millersville, Pa.

HARBY, MRS. LEE COHEN, The Hollies, Conway, S. C.

HARDEN, WILLIAM, 226 President St., West, Savannah, Ga.

HARDING, ALBERT SPENCER, A. M., Professor South Dakota Agricultural College, Brookings, S. D.

HARDING, SAMUEL BANNISTER, Ph. D., Professor Indiana State University, Bloomington, Ind.

HARDING, WILLIAM FLETCHER, Ph. M., 2210 First St., N. W., Washington, D. C.

HARJES, HELEN G., Narberth, Pa.

HARLAN, EDGAR R., Keosauqua, Iowa.

HARLEY, LEWIS R., Central High School, Philadelphia, Pa.

HARNETT, MISS JANE E., Long Beach, Cal. (Pacific Coast Branch.)

HARRIS, DWIGHT J., 1415 Chicago Ave., Evanston, Ill.

HARRIS HENRY R., Marquette, Mich.

HARRIS, JOHN T., B. L., First National Bank Building, Harrisonburg, Va.

HARRIS, NORMAN DWIGHT, Ph. D., 1207 Maple Ave., Evanston, Ill.

HART, ALBERT BUSHNELL, Ph. D., LL. D., Professor Harvard University, Cambridge, Mass.

HART, CHARLES HENRY, LL. B., 2206 Delancy Place, Philadelphia, Pa.

HART, MARY PUTNAM (Mrs. Albert Bushnell), 19 Cragie St:, Cambridge Mass.

HART, SAMUEL, D. D., D. C. L., Vice-Dean and Professor Berkeley Divinity School; President Connesticut Historical Society; Registrar Diocese of Connecticut, Middletown, Conn.

HART, W. O., 134 Carondelet St., New Orleans, La.

HARTE, ARCHIBALD C., Young Men's Christian Association, Mobile, Ala.

HARVEY, CHARLES M., 3825 Westminster Place, *Globe Democrat* Office, St. Louis, Mo.

HASCALL, THEODORUS BAILEY, Ph. D., First Assistant High School, 189 Broad St., Newark, N. J.

HASKELL, DANIEL CARL, Box 62, South Vernon, Vt.

HASKINS, CHARLES HOMER, Ph. D., Professor Harvard University, 15 Prescott Hall, Cambridge, Mass.

HASSE, MISS ADELAIDE R., New York Public Library, 40 Lafayette Place New York, N. Y.

HASTINGS, LEMUEL S., Hanover, N. H.

HATCH, LOUIS CLINTON, A. M., Ph. D., 18 North High St., Bangor, Me.

HAWLEY, WILLIS CHATMAN, A. M., LL. B., Member of Congress of the United States, Salem, Oregon. (Pacific Coast Branch.)

HAWORTH, PAUL LELAND, A. B., A. M., 527 W. 124th St., New York, N. Y.

HAYDEN, REV. HORACE EDWIN, A. M., Corresponding Secretary and Librarian Wyoming Historical and Geological Society, Wilkes-Barre, Pa.

HAYNES, FRED EMORY, Ph. D., Professor Morningside College, 709 Tenth St., Sioux City, Iowa.

HAYNES, GEORGE HENRY, Ph. D., Professor Worcester Polytechnic Institute, Worcester, Mass.

HAYNES, HENRY WILLIAMSON, A. M., Corresponding Secretary Massachusetts Historical Scoiety, 239 Beacon St., Boston. Mass.

HAYES, SARAH J., 297 Claremont Ave., Chicago, Ill.

HAZARD, MISS BLANCHE EVANS, 14 Fayette St., Cambridge, Mass.

HAZARD, CAROLINE, M. A., Litt. D., President Wellesley College, Wellesley, Mass.

HAZELTINE, HAROLD DEXTER, A. B., LL. B., Warren, Pa.

HAZEN, AZEL WASHBURN, D. D., President Middlesex County Historical Society, Middletown, Conn.

HAZEN, CHARLES DOWNER, Ph. D., Professor Smith College, Northampton, Mass.

HEAD, FRANKLIN HARVEY, LL. D., 2 Banks St., Chicago, Ill.

HEALEY, JAMES REDMOND, M. D., 226 East 116th St., New York, N. Y.

HEALY, PATRICK J., Catholic University, Washington, D. C.

HEARON, MISS CLEO, A. B., Ph. B., Mississippi College for Women, Columbus, Miss.

HECKENDORF, WALTER C., 2046 Emerson St., Denver, Col.

HECKER, COL. FRANK J., Detroit, Mich.

HELLER, GEORGE, 1115 N. Sixth St., Sheboygan, Wis.

HELBIG, RICHARD ERNEST, Lenox Library Building, New York, N. Y.

HEMPSTED, MISS JOANNA K., 483 Third Ave., Detroit, Mich.

HENDERSON, ERNEST FLAGG, Ph. D., L. H. D., care Henderson & Co., 24 Nassau St., New York, N. Y.

HENDERSON, JOHN BROOKS, JR., 1720 Rhode Island Ave.,Washington,D.C.

HENNEMAN, JOHN BELL, Ph. D., Professor University of the South Sewanee, Tenn.

HENRY, MISS HARRIET E., 328 French St., Fall River, Mass.

HENRY, REV. H. T., Litt. D., President Roman Catholic High School, Philadelphia, Pa.

HENSEL, W. U., A. M., Lancaster, Pa.

HERBERT, JOHN CURTIS, Mississippi Agricultural and Mechanical College, Agricultural College, Miss.

HERRICK, CHEESMAN ABIAH, Central High School, Philadelphia, Pa.

HERRICK, MYRON T., Cleveland, Ohio.

HERSHEY, AMOS SHARTLE, Ph. D., Professor Indiana State University, Bloomington, Ind.

HERST, HERMAN, JR., B. S., LL. B., 119 Nassau St., New York, N. Y.

HERTELL, ARTHUR F., Phillips Academy, Exeter, N. H.

HESS, WALTER LEON, A. B., 307 W. 86th St., New York, N. Y.

HEWITT, GEO. P., 650 Lowe St., Appleton, Wis.

HICKMAN, MISS EMILY, A. B., 1268 Main St., Buffalo, N. Y.

HIGGINSON, FRANCIS LEE, A. B., 274 Beacon St., Boston, Mass.

HIGGINSON, JAMES JACKSON, A. B., 16 E. 41st St., New York, N. Y.

HIGGINSON, THOMAS WENTWORTH, A. M., LL. D., Cambridge, Mass.

HILDT, JOHN COFFEY, Ph. D., Instructor in History, Smith College, Northampton, Mass.

HILL, ALBERT CLARK, Ph. D., Department of Public Instruction, Albany, N. Y.

HILL, HON. DAVID JAYNE, LL. D., American Minister, The Hague, Netherlands.

HILL, EDWARD EMORY, 5411 Greenwood Ave., Chicago, Ill.

HILL, DON GLEASON, LL. B., A. M.; Dedham, Mass.

HILL, CAPTAIN FREDERIC STANHOPE, 23 Buckingham St., Cambridge, Mass.

HILL, HENRY EVELETH, LL. B., 314 Main St., Worcester, Mass.

HILL, JOHN PHILIP, A. B., 56 Central Savings Bank Building, Baltimore, Md.

HILL, MISS MABEL, 4 Park St., Lowell, Mass.

HILL MEMORIAL LIBRARY, Louisiana State University, Baton Rouge, La.

HILL, WALKER, care American Exchange Bank, St. Louis, Mo.

HILLARD, MISS MARY R., Principal St. Margaret's School, Waterbury, Conn.

HILTON, HENRY H., 378 Wabash Ave., Chicago, Ill.

HIMES, GEORGE H., Assistant Secretary and Curator, Oregon Historical Society, City Hall, Portland, Ore. (Pacific Coast Branch.)

HITCHCOCK, RIPLEY, A. B., The Strathmore, Broadway and 52d St., New York, N. Y.

HOAR, D. BLAKELY, 100 High St., Brookline, Mass.

HOBE, MISS SOPHIE A., 604 Capp St., San Francisco, Cal. (Pacific Coast Branch.)

HOCKETT, HOMER C., B. L., Professor of History and Economics, Central College, Fayette, Mo.

HODDER, FRANK HEYWOOD, Ph. M., Professor of American History, University of Kansas, Lawrence, Kan.

HODDER, MRS. MABEL E., M. A., Wellesley College, 24 Irving St., Cambridge, Mass.

HODENPYL, ANTON GYSBERTI, care Hodenpyl, Walbridge & Co., 7 Wall St., New York, N. Y.

HODGE, FREDERICK WEBB, Editor "American Anthropologist," Bureau of American Ethnology, Washington, D. C.

HODGIN, CYRUS WILBURN, A. M., Professor Earlham College, Richmond, Ind.

HOERMANN, PROF. ARTHUR, Ph. D., Northwestern University, Watertown, Wis.

HOFER, MISS ELIZABETH J., Pd. M., 142 W. 11th St., New York City.

HOLDOM, JUDGE JESSE, Superior Court of Cook County, Chicago, Ill.

HOLLIS, JOHN PORTER, Ph. D., Southwestern University, Georgetown, Tex.

HOLLISTER, CLAY HARVEY, A. B., Grand Rapids, Mich.

HOLMESLEY, GEORGIA ANN, Clifton, Ariz.

HOLMAN, FREDERICK VAN VOORHIES, P. O. Box 504, Portland, Ore. (Pacific Coast Branch.)

HOLMES, MRS. ALBERT W., 1890 West Carmen Ave., Chicago, Ill.

HOLT, CHARLES SUMNER, A. B., 131 La Salle St., Chicago, Ill.

HOLT, WILLIAM ARTHUR, Oconto, Wis.

HOOSE, JAMES HARMON, A. M., Ph. D., Department of History and Philosophy (University of Southern California), University Station, Los Angeles, Cal. (Pacific Coast Branch.)

*HOPKINS, GEORGE BATES, 52 Broadway, New York, N. Y.

HORNE, CHARLES F., M. S., 17 Lexington Ave., New York, N. Y.

HORNE, PERLEY LEONARD, A. M., President Kamehameha Schools, Honolulu, Hawaii.

HORNER, J. B., Professor of History, Oregon Agricultural College, Corvallis, Ore.

HORR, REV. GEORGE EDWIN, A. M., D. D., 63 Institution Ave., Newton Centre, Mass.

HORTON, HORACE E., Proprietor Chicago Bridge & Iron Works, Washington Heights Station, Chicago, Ill.

HORTON, KATHARINE PRATT (Mrs. John M.), 477 Delaware Ave., Buffalo, N. Y.

HOSMER, HON. GEORGE S., Detroit, Mich.

HOSMER, JAMES KENDALL, A. B., A. M., Ph. D., LL. D., 47 Court St., Boston, Mass.

HOTCHKISS, FRANK E., Yale University, New Haven, Conn.

HOUGHTON, CLEMENT STEVENS, 191 Commonwealth Ave., Boston, Mass.

HOUSE, MRS. WILLIE DURHAM, A. M., Librarian Waco Public Library, cor. 12th and Austin Ave., Waco, Tex.

HOWARD, GEORGE ELLIOTT, Ph. D., University of Nebraska, 1910 E St., Lincoln, Neb.

HOWARD, JAMES Q., Library of Congress, Washington, D. C.

HOWARD, JOEL T., Dallas, Tex.

HOWE, MISS AGNES EMMONS, A. B., State Normal School, San Jose, Cal. (Pacific Coast Branch.)

HOWE, EDMUND GRANT, 28 Conant Hall, Cambridge, Mass.

HOWE, HERBERT CROMBIE, 908 Alder St., Eugene, Ore. (Pacific Coast Branch.)

HOWE, MARK ANTONY DE WOLFE, 26 Brimmer St., Boston, Mass.

HOWE, WINFRED CHESTER, 2302 Prairie Ave., Milwaukee, Wis.

HOWE, HON. WILLIAM WIRT, LL. D., A. M., 708 Union St., New Orleans, La.

HOWELL, SELAH, A. M., Boston Latin School, 9 Kirk St., West Roxbury, Mass.

HOWEY, MRS. LAURA E., A. M., Secretary and Librarian Montana State Library, Helena, Mont. (Pacific Coast Branch.)

HOWISON, GEORGE HOLMES, M. A., LL. D., Professor of Philosophy University of California, 2731 Bancroft Way, Berkeley, Cal. (Pacific Coast Branch.)

HOWLAND, ARTHUR CHARLES, Ph. D., University of Pennsylvania, Philahelphia, Pa.

HUBBARD, E. KENT, JR., B. S., " Arawana," Middletown, Conn.

HUBBARD, LUCIUS, 117 E. Madison St., South Bend, Ind.

HUBBARD, LUCIUS LEE, Ph. D., Houghton, Mich.

HUBBARD, WALTER BULKLEY, 115 Main St., Middletown, Conn.

HUDSON, GARDNER KIRK, 2 Park Building, Fitchburg, Mass.

HUDSON, RICHARD, A. M., Professor University of Michigan, Ann Arbor, Mich.

HUFF, JOSEPH W., 930 East Chelton St., Philadelphia, Pa.

HUFFCUT, ERNEST WILSON, Cornell University College of Law, Ithaca, N. Y.

HUGHES, ADRIAN, 223 St. Paul St., Baltimore, Md.

HUGHES, HARRIET LOUISE, B. L., 746 Algoma St., Oshkosh, Wis.

HUGHES, PERCY M., Assistant Superintendent Public Schools, Washington, D. C.

HUHNER, LEON, A. M., LL. B., 5 Beekman St., New York, N. Y.

HULBERT, ERI BAKER, D. D., LL. D., University of Chicago, Chicago, Ill.

HULBERT, HENRY WOODWARD, A. M., D. D., Bangor, Me.

HULING, RAY GREENE, Sc. D., Head Master English High School, 17 Hurlbut St., Cambridge, Mass.

HULL, CHARLES HENRY, Ph. D., Professor Cornell University, Ithaca, N. Y.

HULL, MISS GERTRUDE, Teacher in English, West Division High School, 2009 State St., Milwaukee, Wis.

HULL, WILLIAM ISAAC, Ph. D., Professor Swarthmore College, Swarthmore, Pa.

HULME, EDWARD MASLIN, University of Idaho, Moscow, Idaho. (Pacific Coast Branch.)

HULST, NELSON POWELL, A. B., Ph. B., Ph. D., Milwaukee, Wis.

HUMPHREY, MISS MARY H., Ph. B., High School, Simsbury, Conn.

HUNSICKER, JOHN R., Superintendent of Schools, Dowington, Pa.

HUNT, GAILLARD, Department of State, Washington, D. C.

HUNT, ROCKWELL DENNIS, Ph. D., Principal of High School, 624 Myrtle St., San Jose, Cal. (Pacific Coast Branch.)

*HUNTINGTON, ARCHER M., A. M., Hispanic Society Building, 156th St., West of Broadway, New York, N. Y.

HURLSTONE, ALBERT, Pastor Roberts Park Methodist Church, Indianapolis, Ind.

HUTCHINGS, MRS. JAMES M., 910 Devisadero St., San Francisco, Cal.

HUTCHINS, JERE CHAMBERLAIN, Detroit, Mich.

HUTCHINSON, CHARLES L., 2709 Prairie Ave., Chicago, Ill.

HUTCHINSON, PROF. LINCOLN, Faculty Club, Berkeley, Cal. (Pacific Coast Branch.)

HUTH, CARL F., 557 West 124th St., New York, N. Y,

HUTSON, CHARLES WOODWARD, A. M., College of Texas, College Station, Texas.

HUTTMANN, MAUDE A., 417 West 118th St., New York, N. Y.

HYDE, ARTHUR MAY, A. M., 1601 Boswell Ave., Topeka, Kan.

HYDE, HARRIET COURTNEY, Middle Haddam, Conn.

HYDE, REV. J. CHESTER, The Baptist Parsonage, 1 Free St., Dexter, Me.

*HYDE, JAMES H., President " Federation des Alliances Francaises," 120 Broadway, New York, N. Y.

*ILES, GEORGE, Park Avenue Hotel, New York, N. Y., (June 1 to Oct. 1, care of Carnegie Library, Ottawa, Ontario, Can.)

ILES, I. VICTOR, A. M., 430 Francis St., Madison, Wis.

ILLINOIS STATE NORMAL UNIVERSITY, Normal, Ill.

INDIANA STATE UNIVERSITY LIBRARY, Bloomington, Ind.

INGALSBE, HON. GRENVILLE MELLEN, A. M., LL. B., 16 Pearl St., Sandy Hill, N. Y.

*INGRAM, O. H., Eau Claire, Wis.

INSKEEP, LORENZO D., A. M., 1050 E. 30th St., Oakland, Cal. (Pacific Coast Branch.)

IOWA STATE COLLEGE LIBRARY, Ames, Iowa.

IRWIN, MISS SOPHY DALLAS, 2011 De Lancey Place, Philadelphia, Pa.

ISAACS, STANLEY MYER, A. M., LL. B., 52 William St., New York, N. Y.

ISELY, W. H., Dean of Fairmount College, Wichita, Kan.

ISHAM, CHARLES, A. B., Room 1801, 27 William St., New York, N. Y.

JACKSON, ALFRED AUGUSTUS, A. M., Janesville, Wis.

JACKSON, CAROLINE COOKE, B. S., 1379 Eighth Ave., East Oakland, Cal.

*JACKSON, SAMUEL MACAULEY, D. D., LL. D., 692 West End Ave., New York, N. Y.

JACOB TOME INSTITUTE, Port Deposit, Md.

JACOBS, HENRY BARTON, A. B., M. D., 11 Mt. Vernon Place, West, Baltimore, Md.

JACOBS, HENRY EYSTER, D. D., LL. D., Mt. Airy, Philadelphia, Pa.

JAMES, EDWARD W., 34 Fenchurch St., Norfolk, Va.

JAMES, JAMES ALTON, Ph. D., Professor Northwestern University, Evanston, Ill.

*JAMESON, JOHN FRANKLIN, Ph. D., LL. D., Carnegie Institution, Washington, D. C.

*JANNEY, ROBERT M., 112 Drexel Bldg:, Philadelphia, Pa.

JARVES, DEMING, Santa Barbara, Cal.

JEFFERSON, MISS LORIAN P., Baraboo, Wis.

JENKINS, E. AUSTIN, 1300 St. Paul St., Baltimore, Md.

JENCKES, ADALINE, Buttercup Cottage, Gresheimer Road, Mt. Airy, Pa.

JENKINS, CHARLES FRANCIS, Box 1632, Philadelphia, Pa.

JENKINS, MISS MABEL IRENE, State Normal Training School, Willimantic, Conn.

*JENKS, REV. HENRY FITCH, A. M., Recording Secretary of the Prince Society, Canton Junction, Mass.

JENNE, MRS. M. E., Pullman, Wash.   (Pacific Coast Branch.)

JENNINGS, ALBERT, B. S., LL. B., Union High School, Grand Rapids, Mich.

JENNISON, REV. JOSEPH F. 1306 Madison Ave., Baltimore, Md.

JERNEGAN, MARCUS WILSON, A. M., Edgartown, Mass.

JEROME, THOMAS SPENCER, A. M., Villa Castello, Capri, Italy.

JOHNSON, ALLEN, Ph. D., Bowdoin College, Brunswick, Me.

JOHNSON, BENJAMIN FRANKLIN, 945 Pa. Ave., N. W., Washington, D. C.

JOHNSON, CARMAN C., Juniata College, Huntington, Pa.

JOHNSON, HENRY, A. M., Professor of History, Teachers College, Columbia University, 2881 Broadway, New York, N. Y.

JOHNSON, HENRY C., Decorah City Schools, Decorah, Iowa.

JOHNSON, MISS LILLIAN WYCKOFF, Ph. D., The Western College, Oxford, Ohio.

JOHNSON, LUCY H., A. M., Kalamazoo College, Kalamazoo, Mich.

JOHNSON, THOMAS CARY, A. B., S. D., LL. D., Richmond, Va.

JOHNSON, MISS WINIFRED, A. B., Head of Department of History, State Normal School, Cape Girardeau, Mo.

JOHNSTON, JOSEPH M., 200 W. Clinton St., Cleveland, Ohio.

JOHNSTON, R. M., 44 Shepard St., Cambridge, Mass.

JOHNSTON, SAMUEL RUTHERFORD, 415 12th St., Portland, Ore.   (Pacific Coast Branch.)

JOLINE, ADRIAN HOFFMAN, LL. B., LL. D., A. M., 54 Wall St., New York, N. Y.

JONES, BRECKINRIDGE, 45 Portland Place, St. Louis, Mo.

JONES, FERNANDO, 1834 Prairie Ave., Chicago, Ill.

JONES, FREDERICK ROBERTSON, Ph. D., Bryn Mawr College, Low Bldg., Bryn Mawr, Pa.

JONES, GUERNSEY, Ph. D., Professor University of Nebraska, Lincoln, Neb.

JONES, JAMES K., 915 M St., Washington, D. C.

*JONES, MISS M. LOUISE, A. M., State Normal School, Emporia, Kan.

JONES, J. WILLIAM, D. D., Superintendent and Secretary Confederate Memorial Association, 709½ West Clay St., Richmond, Va.

JOPLING, ALFRED OWEN, Marquette, Mich.

JOPLING, JAMES EDMUND, Marquette, Mich.

JORDAN, EDITH MONICA, Stanford University, Cal. (Pacific Coast Branch.)

JORDAN, FRITZ HERMANN, Treasurer Maine Historical Society, Portland, Me.

JOSSELYN, HOMER WALKER, 112 Pingree Ave., Detroit, Mich.

JOUROLMON, LEON, 24-26 Deaderick Bldg., Knoxville, Tenn.

JUDSON, HARRY PRATT, LL. D., Professor University of Chicago, Chicago, Ill.

JUDSON, LEULAH, A. B., A. M., University of Minnesota, Minneapolis, Minn.

JUPP, MISS SARAH S. ELIZABETH, B. A., M. A., 523 Washington Ave., Brooklyn, N. Y.

JUSTICE, MISS ANNA, 2025 Pine St., Philadelphia, Pa.

KABEL, PHILIP, President Randolph County Historical Society, Winchester, Ind.

KANE, ELIZABETH GALLOWAY, A. B., 155 Cherry St., Waterbury, Conn.

KANSAS STATE HISTORICAL SOCIETY, Topeka, Kan.

KANSAS STATE UNIVERSITY LIBRARY, University of Kansas, Lawrence, Kan.

KATZENBERGER, GEORGE ANTHONY, LL. B., Greenville, Ohio.

KAYE, PERCY L., Ph. D., Johns Hopkins University, Baltimore, Md.

*KEACH, MISS MARY A., 102 Williams St., Providence, R. I.

KEEFE, MISS ANNA, 267 S. 8th St., San Jose, Cal. (Pacific Coast Branch.)

KEENE, FRANCIS B., A. B., U. S. Consul, Geneva, Switzerland.

KEEP, CHAUNCEY, Room 901, 135 Adams St., Chicago, Ill.

KEISTER, A. L., First National Bank, Scottdale, Pa.

KEITH, ELBRIDGE GERRY, 1900 Prairie Ave., Chicago, Ill.

KELKER, LUTHER R., 128 Walnut St., Harrisburg, Pa.

KELLEN, WILLIAM VAIL, Ph. D., 202 Commonwealth Ave., Boston, Mass.

KELLEY, CAPT. JAMES MUNGER, Tiburon, Cal.

KELLOGG, MISS LOUISE PHELPS, B. L., Ph. D., Manuscript Department Wisconsin Historical Library, Madison, Wis.

*KELSEY, FRANCIS WILLEY, Ph. D., Professor University of Michigan, Ann Arbor, Mich.

KELSEY, R. W., Whittier, Cal. (Pacific Coast Branch.)

KELSO, MISS INEZ FANNIE, Humestown, Iowa.

KENDALL, MISS ELIZABETH KIMBALL, M. A., Associate Professor Wellesley College, Wellesley, Mass.

KENDALL, W. KING, Eugene, Ore. (Pacific Coast Branch.)

KENT, CHARLES ARTEMAS, LL. D., Detroit, Mich.

KENT, GEORGE H., Justice of the Peace, Suffolk, Miss.

KENYON, MISS ELIZABETH WATSON, A. M., University of Wisconsin, Madison, Wis.

KEOGH, ANDREW, A. M., Yale University Library, New Haven, Conn.

KERFOOT, SAMUEL H., JR., Chamber of Commerce, Chicago, Ill.

KERR, MRS. ALICE M., Catonsville, Md.

KERSHOW, CARLTON MONTGOMERY, B. S., 2019 Spruce St., Philadelphia, Pa.

KEYS, ALICE M., Ph. D., 267 West 90th St., New York, N. Y.

KIDDER, ALFRED, 183 Brattle St., Cambridge, Mass.

KIDGER, HORACE, A. M., Aberdeen, South Dakota.

KIEFER, Hon. HERMANN, 89 E. Forest Ave., Detroit, Mich.

KIENTZLE, JOHN PHILIP, 256 E. 11th St., Erie, Pa.

KILGORE, MISS CARRIE B., A. M., Swarthmore, Pa.

KILLIKELLY, MISS SARAH HUTCHINS, 171 W. 95th St., New York, N. Y.

KIMBALL, MISS EDITH M., Ph. B., 348 Islington St., Toledo, Ohio.

KIMBALL, EVERETT, Ph. D., 15 Franklin St., Northampton, Mass.

KIMBALL, MISS GERTRUDE SELWYN, 263 Benefit St., Providence, R. I.

KING, MISS ALICE, Coe College, Cedar Rapids, Iowa.

KING, MISS HARRIET G., A. M., Scoville Place, Oak Park, Ill.

KING, JULIA ANNE, A. M., Professor State Normal College, Ypsilanti, Mich.

KINGSBURY, MISS SUSAN M., A. M., Riverbank Court, Cambridge, Mass.

KINNEY, BURT ORNON, 607 So. Spring St., Los Angeles, Cal. (Pacific Coast Branch.)

KINNEY, S. WARDWELL, Country School for Boys, Baltimore, Md.

KINZER, STUART L. B., 83 E. Baltimore Ave., Lansdowne, Delaware Co., Pa.

KIRCHNER, OTTO, A. M., 80 Griswold St., Detroit, Mich.

KITTLE, WILLIAM, Madison, Wis.

KLEIN, JULIUS, Canyon Road, Berkeley, Cal. (Pacific Coast Branch.)

KLINE, VIRGIL P., Cleveland, Ohio.

KNELL, MRS. JOHN, 1460 Clay St., San Francisco, Cal. (Pacific Coast Branch.)

KNEELAND, FRANK G., St. Louis, Mich.

KNIESS, MRS. LYDIA HEBRON, Niles, Cal. (Pacific Coast Branch.)

*KNIGHT, GEORGE WELLS, Ph. D., Professor Ohio State University, Columbus, Ohio.

KNOWLAND, HON. J. R., House of Representatives, Washington, D. C. (Pacific Coast Branch.)

KNOWLES, MISS ANTOINETTE, College Park, San Jose, Cal. (Pacific Coast Branch.)

KNOWLTON, DANIEL CHAUNCEY, A. B., care Montclair High School, 99 Valley Road, Montclair, N. J.

KNOTT, HON. ALOYSIUS LEO, LL. D., 1029 St. Paul St., Baltimore, Md.

KNOX, MISS FRANCES ADA, Box 32, Faculty Exchange, University of Chicago, Chicago, Ill.

KNOX, REV. P. B., Rector St. Patrick's Church, Madison, Wis.

KOCH, THEODORE WESLEY, Librarian University of Michigan, Ann Arbor, Mich.

KOCHENDERFER, CLARENCE C., Olivet College, Olivet, Mich.

KOHLER, HON. MAX JAMES, LL. B., 42 Broadway, New York, N. Y.

KOHLSAAT, HERMANN H., 120 Lake Shore Drive, Chicago, Ill.

KONKLE, BURTON ALVA, Swarthmore, Pa.

KOONS, GUY J., Superintendent of Schools, Mason City, Ill.

KRAMER, MISS STELLA, M. A., 311 West 111th St., New York, N. Y.

KREHBIEL, EDWARD B., A. B., 445 East 56th St., Chicago, Ill.

KRIEHN, GEORGE, Ph. D., 408 Manhattan Ave., New York, N. Y.

KROTEL, GOTTLOB FREDERICK, D. D., LL. D., 65 Convent Ave., New York, N. Y.

KRUEGER, REV. FREDERIC TEVIS, M. A., S. T. B., Sterling, Colo.

KRUMWEIDE, WALTER, 132 West 83rd St., New York, N. Y.

KUHLMANN, DR. CHARLES, Joliet, Mont.

KUHN, MISS HELEN B., Department of History, Smith College, Wallace House, Northampton, Mass.

LACHMAN, HON. SAMSON, A. B., LL. B., 313 West 106th St., New York.

LACOCK, JOHN KENNEDY, A. B., 21 Carver St., Cambridge, Mass.

LACONIA PUBLIC LIBRARY, Laconia, N. H.

LADD, HORATIO OLIVER, A. M., S. T. D., 62 Clinton Ave., Jamaica, N. Y.

LADD, PROFESSOR W. P., Berkeley Divinity School, Middletown, Conn.

LAMBERT, MAJOR WILLIAM H., 330 W. Johnson St., Germantown, Philadelphia, Pa.

LAMBERTON, JAMES M., A. B., 216 Market St., Harrisburg, Pa.

LAMONTE, GEORGE M., Littlegrange, Bound Brook, N. J.

LAMPE, JOSEPH JOACHIM, Ph. D., D. D., 4824 Davenport St., Omaha, Neb.

LAMPRECHT, KARL G., Professor of History, University of Leipzig, Leipzig, Germany.

*LANDFIELD, JEROME BARKER, A. B., University of California, Berekley, Cal. (Pacific Coast Branch.)

LANE, ISAAC REMSEN, 325 Lincoln Ave., Orange, N. J.

LANE, WILLIAM COOLIDGE, A. B., Librarian Harvard University Library, Cambridge, Mass.

LANGDON, WILLIAM CHAUNCY, A. M., District Attorney's Office, Criminal Court Bldg., New York, N. Y.

LANSING, GERRIT YATES, 82 State St., Albany, N. Y.

LAPSLEY, GAILLARD THOMAS, Ph. D., Trinity College, Cambridge, England.

LARNED, JOSEPHUS NELSON, A. M., 35 Johnson Park, Buffalo, N. Y.

LARSON, LAWRENCE M., Ph. D., East Division High School, 352 Farwell Ave., Milwaukee, Wis.

LARZELERE, CLAUDE S., A. M., Professor Central State Normal School, Mt. Pleasant, Mich.

LATANÉ, JOHN HOLLADAY, Ph. D., Washington and Lee University, Lexington, Va.

LATHROP, ADELE, Horace Mann School, 120th St., W., New York, N. Y.

LAUNDON, MORTIMER H., care Society for Savings, Cleveland, Ohio.

LAUT, MISS AGNES C., Wildwood Place, Wassaic, N. Y.

LAW, JESSIE MAY, Ph. D., 26 Greenleaf St., Springfield, Mass.

LAWFORD, JASPER M., 718 N. Howard St., Baltimore, Md.

LAWHEAD, MRS. LYDIA D., B. L., Woodland, Cal. (Pacific Coast Branch.)

LAWRENCE, DANIEL WINSLOW, B. S., Principal of Northbranch Academy, Northbranch, Kan.

LAWTON, ALEXANDER RUDOLPH, Savannah, Ga.

*LEA, HENRY CHARLES, LL. D., Vice-President Historical Society of Pennsylvania, 2000 Walnut St., Philadelphia, Pa.

LEADBETTER, FLORENCE EUGENIE, Roxbury High School, Boston, Mass.

LEAKE, GEN. JOSEPH B., 99 Washington St., Chicago, Ill.

LEAKIN, J. WILSON, 705 Fidelity Building, Baltimore, Md.

LEAR, J. MERRITT, Charlottesville, Va.

*LEARNED, DWIGHT WHITNEY, Ph. D., D. D., Kioto, Japan.

LEARNED, HENRY BARRETT, A. M., 204 Prospect St., New Haven, Conn.

LEARNED, M. D., Department of Philosophy, University of Pennsylvania, Philadelphia, Pa.

*LEAVENWORTH, CHARLES SAMUEL, A. B., care of Brown, Shipley & Co., 123 Pall Mall, London, S. W., England.

LEAVITT, MISS BLANCHE, Ph. B., Department of History, Rogers High School, 14 Malborn Road, Newport, R. I.

LEE, CHARLES HENRY, LL. B., Racine, Wis.

*Lee, EDWARD CLINTON, Haverford, Pa.

LEE, GEORGE WASHINGTON CUSTIS, LL. D., Burke, Va.

LEE, GUY CARLETON, Ph. D., Johns Hopkins University, Baltimore, Md.

LEE, JOHN PAUL, 3159 Bert St., Denver, Col.

LEE, JOHN THOMAS, care of Dept. of State, Madison, Wis.

LEE LIBRARY ASSOCIATION, Lee, Mass.

LEE, STEPHEN, D., LL. D., Columbus, Miss.

LEGLER, HENRY E., Free Library Commission, Madison, Wis.

LEIPZIGER, HENRY MARCUS, Ph. D., Board of Education, 59th St. and Park Ave., New York, N. Y.

LELAND STANFORD JUNIOR UNIVERSITY (History Department), Stanford, University, Cal.

LELAND, WALDO GIFFORD, A. M., Carnegie Institution of Washington, Washington, D. C.

LEONARD, MISS MARY ANDERSON, Ph. B., Greer, S. C.

LEONARD, RT. REV. WILLIAM ANDREW, D. D., Bishop of Ohio, Cleveland, Ohio.

LE ROY, JAMES A., American Consul, Durango, Mexico.

LESEM, JOSAPHINE, 5720 Calumet Ave., Chicago, Ill.

LESTER, MAXWELL, 30 Broad St., New York, N. Y.

LEVERMORE, CHARLES HERBERT, Ph. D., President Adelphi College, Brooklyn, N. Y.

LEWINTHAL, RABBI ISADORE, 1912 West End Ave., Nashville, Tenn.

LEWIS, ABRAM HERBERT, D. D., LL. D., 633 W. 7th St., Plainfield, N. J.

LEWIS, ERNEST DORMAN, High School of Commerce, 155 West 65th St., New York, N. Y.

LEWIS, HARRY BLAKEMAN, Ph. B., P. O. Box 12, Indianapolis, Ind.

LEWIS, HOMER PIERCE, Superintendent of Schools, 3 Monadnock Road, Worcester, Mass.

LEWIS INSTITUTE, Chicago, Ill.

*LEWIS, ISAAC NEWTON, A. B., A. M., LL. B., East Walpole, Mass.

LEWIS, JESSE, A. B., State Normal School, Maryville, Mo.

LEWIS, LESTAN L., 183 E. 12th St., Eugene, Ore. (Pacific Coast Branch.)

LEWIS, MISS SARAH, B. D., A. M., 220 Walnut St., Brookline, Mass.

LEWIS, VIRGIL A., M. A., State Historian and Archivist, Charleston, W. Va.

LIBBY, PROFESSOR ARTHUR S., A. M., Converse College, Spartanburg, S. C.

LIBBY, ORIN GRANT, Ph. D., Professor University of North Dakota, Grand Forks, N. Dak.

LIBRARY ASSOCIATION OF PORTLAND, Portland, Ore.

LIBRARY OF NEW YORK UNIVERSITY, University Heights, New York City.

LIBRARY OF PARLIMENT, Ottawa, Ontario, Canada.

LIBRARY OF THE UNIVERSITY OF GEORGIA, Athens, Ga.

LICHTENSTEIN, WALTER, A. B., A. M., 29 Wendell St., Cambridge, Mass.

LIGHTNER, CLARENCE A., Detroit, Mich.

LIGHTNER, WILLIAM HURLEY, A. B., St. Paul, Minn.

LINCOLN, CHARLES HENRY, Ph. D., " The Roland," 2d and B Sts., N. E., Washington, D. C.

LINCOLN LIBRARY, Springfield, Ill.

LINCOLN, SOLOMON, A. M., LL. B., 53 State St., Boston, Mass.

LINCOLN CITY LIBRARY, Lincoln, Neb.

LINDLEY, HARLOW, A. M., Librarian and Professor of History, Earlham College, Richmond, Ind.

LINDSEY, EDWARD, Warren, Pa.

LINES, EDWIN STEVENS, D. D., 21 Washington St., Newark, N. J.

LINGELBACH, WILLIAM EZRA, Ph. D., College Hall, University of Pennsylvania, Philadelphia, Pa.

LINGLEY, CHARLES RAMSDELL, B. S., A. M., Jacob Tome Institute, Port Deposit, Md.

LIPMAN, FREDERICK LOCKWOOD, care Wells, Fargo & Co. Bank, San Francisco, Cal. (Pacific Coast Branch.)

LITTLE, GEORGE THOMAS, Litt. D., Librarian Bowdoin College, Brunswick, Me.

LLOYD, ALFRED HENRY, Ph. D., Professor of Philosophy, Ann Arbor, Mich.

LOCKWOOD, MRS. MARY S., The Columbia, Columbia Heights, Washington, D. C.

LOEB, ISIDOR, Ph. D., Professor University of the State of Missouri, Columbia, Mo.

LOEWY, BENNO, LL. B., 206 Broadway, New York.

LOGAN, JOHN P., P. O. Box 392, West Chester, Pa.

LOGANSPORT PUBLIC LIBRARY (Elizabeth McCullough, Librarian), Logansport, Ind.

LOMBARD, J. W. P., National Exchange Bank, Milwaukee, Wis.

LONGSTRETH, EMMA J., 5304 Spruce St., Philadelphia, Pa.

LONGYEAR, HON. JOHN MUNRO, Marquette, Mich.

LOOKER, OSCAR REAM, care Mutual Life Ins. Co., Detroit, Mich.

LOOMIS, JOHN H., 222 Ashland Boulevard, Chicago, Ill.

LOOMIS, MISS LOUISE ROPES, Ph. D., Cornell University, Ithaca, N. Y.

LORD, ARTHUR, A. B., Plymouth, Mass.

LORD, MISS CHARLOTTE MABEL, A. B., A. M., Palo Alto, Cal. (Pacific Coast Branch.)

LORD, DANIEL M., Vice-President Metropolitan Trust and Savings Bank, 5450 Cornell Ave., Chicago, Ill.

LORD, MISS ELEANOR LOUISA, Ph. D., Woman's College, Baltimore, Md.

LORD, LIVINGSTONE C., President Eastern Illinois State Normal School, Charleston, Ill.

LORING, ARTHUR, 16 Spring Park Ave., Jamaica Plain, Mass.

LORING, HON. WILLIAM CALEB, A. M., LL. D., 2 Gloucester St., Boston, Mass.

LOS ANGELES STATE NORMAL SCHOOL, Los Angeles, Cal.

LOTHROP, CYRUS E., Detroit, Mich.

LOTHROP, THORNTON KIRKLAND, A. M., LL. B., 27 Commonwealth Ave., Boston, Mass.

LOUGH, SUSIE M., 3812 Michigan Ave., Chicago, Ill.

LOW, J. HERBERT, M. A., 177 Woodruff Ave., Brooklyn, N. Y.

*LOW, HON. SETH, LL. D., New York, N. Y.

LOWBER, JAMES WILLIAM, Ph. D., LL. D., Pastor of Christian Church, 113 E. 18th St., Austin, Tex.

LOWE, WALTER IRENAEUS, Ph. D., Wells College, Aurora, N. Y.

LOWELL, ABBOTT LAWRENCE, A. M., LL. B., 843 Exchange Building, Boston, Mass.

LOWELL, HON. FRANCIS CABOT, A. B., U. S. District Judge, 709 Exchange Building, Boston, Mass.

LOWRY, ROBERT J., Atlanta, Ga.

LUDLOW, JAMES MEEKER, D. D., L. H. D., East Orange, N. J.

LUETSCHER, GEORGE D., B. L., Ph. D., 64 Union Ave., Jamaica, New York, N. Y.

LURTON, FREEMAN ELLSWORTH, M. S., M. A., Ph. D., Superintendent of Schools, Director of Public Library, Fergus Falls, Minn.

LUTHER, OTTO L., Seattle High School, Seattle, Wash. (Pacific Coast Branch.)

LYDENBERG, HARRY MILLER, A. B., New York Public Library, New York, N. Y.

LYLE, EDITH KATHERINE, Milwaukee-Downer College, Milwaukee, Wis.

LYMAN, ARTHUR THEODORE, A. M., P. O. Box 1717, Boston, Mass.

LYMAN, MISS EUNICE ALMENA, B. A., 154 Hanover St., Fall River, Mass.

LYTTLE, EUGENE W., M. A., Ph. D., University of the State of New York, Albany, N. Y.

MACALISTER, JAMES, LL. D., President Drexel Institute, Philadelphia, Pa.

MCANENY, GEORGE, 19 E. 47th St., New York, N. Y.

MCBRIDE, JOHN HARRIS, 1357 Euclid Ave., Cleveland, Ohio.

McCAGG, E. B., 153 La Salle St. Chicago, Ill.

McCALEB, WALTER FLAVIUS, A. M., Ph. D., Carrizo Springs, Tex.

McCALLUM, JAMES S., Eugene, Ore. (Pacific Coast Branch.)

McCARTHY, CHARLES, Ph. D., 421 Murray St., Madison, Wis.

McCARTHY, CHARLES DANIEL, M. D., 164 Pleasant St., Malden, Mass.

McCARTHY, CHARLES H., Ph. D., Department of American History Catholic University of America, Washington, D. C.

McCARTY, DWIGHT G., A. M., LL. B., Emmetsburg, Iowa.

McCLELLAND, THOMAS S., A. B., A. M., 417 Superior St., Chicago, Ill.

McCLENCH, WILLIAM WALLACE, 112 Sumner Ave., Springfield, Mass.

McCLINTOCK, E. E., A. B., College for Women, Columbia, S. C.

McCLURE, SAMUEL S., 141 E. 25th St., New York.

McCOMB, PETER H. K., D. C., Professor of History and Political Science, Hanover College, Hanover, Ind.

MACOMBER, ALBERT E., Spitzer Building, Toledo, Ohio.

McCONNELL, MRS. MATILDA R., 112 Madison Ave., New York, N. Y.

*McCOOK, JOHN JAMES, LL. D., 120 Broadway, New York, N. Y.

McCORDIC, ALFRED E., 329 The Rookery, Chicago, Ill.

McCORMAC, EUGENE IRVING, Ph. D., University of California, Berkeley, Cal. (Pacific Coast Branch.)

McCORMICK, REV. SAMUEL B., D. D., LL. D., Western University of Pennsylvania, Allegheny, Pa.

McCORVEY, THOMAS CHALMERS, A. M., Professor University of Alabama, Tuscaloosa, Ala.

McCOWAN, JOSEPH STEWART, A. M., Iowa College, Grinnell, Iowa.

McCOY, MARGARET, 277 East 55th St., Chicago, Ill.

McCRACKAN, WILLIAM DENISON, A. M., 385 Commonwealth Ave., Boston, Mass.

MacCRACKEN, HENRY MITCHELL, D. D., LL. D., University Heights, New York, N. Y.

MacCRACKEN, JOHN HENRY, Ph. D., LL. D., Syndic New York University, New York, N. Y.

McCREA, SAMUEL P., B. S., A. B., A. M., Principal Sequoia Union High School, Redwood City, Cal. (Pacific Coast Branch.)

McCULLOCH, REV. WILLIAM E., 7133 Race St., Pittsburgh, Pa.

McDANIEL, MISS SYDNIE, 1328 Thirteenth Ave., N., Birmingham, Ala.

McDEVITT, PHILIP R., Supt. Parish Schools, Broad and Vine Sts., Philadelphia, Pa.

MACDONALD, AUGUSTIN SYLVESTER, 508 Union Savings Bank Building, Oakland, Cal. (Pacific Coast Branch.)

MacDONALD, WILLIAM, Ph. D., LL. D., 450 Brook St., Providence, R. I.

MACE, WILLIAM HARRISON, Ph. D., Professor Syracuse University, 127 College Place, Syracuse, N. Y.

McELROY, ROBERT McNUTT, Ph.D., Princeton University, Princeton, N.J.

McGAW, GEORGE K., Baltimore, Md.

McGIFFERT, ARTHUR CUSHMAN, Ph. D., D. D., 700 Park Ave., New York.

MACGILL, CAROLINE ELIZABETH, care of Stanley Electric Works, Pittsfield, Mass.

McGILL UNIVERSITY LIBRARY, Montreal, Canada.

McGILVRAY, MISS J. D., Box 134 Stanford University, Cal. (Pacific Coast Branch.)

McGLOTHLIN, WILLIAM JOSEPH, Ph. D., Norton Hall, Louisville, Ky.

McGOVNEY, DUDLEY ODELL, 527 W. 124th St., New York, N. Y.

McGUCKIN, WILLIAM G., A. M., LL. B., Assistant Professor of History, College of the City of New York, New York, N. Y.

McHUGH, HON. WILLIAM DOUGLAS, Omaha, Neb.

McILWAIN, CHARLES HOWARD, A. M., Professor Princteon University, 9 Madison St., Princeton, N. J.

MACK, EDWIN S., A. M., LL. B., 403 Lake Drive, Milwaukee, Wis.

MACK, JULIAN WILLIAM, Ph. B., Professor of Law, Judge of Circuit Court, 444 Manadnock Building, Chicago, Ill.

McKEAN COUNTY HISTORICAL SOCIETY, Bradford, Pa.

MACKENZIE, GEORGE NORBURY, LL. B., Attorney at Law, Room 27 Builders Exchange Building, Baltimore, Md.

McKINLEY, ALBERT EDWARD, Ph. D., 6219 Boynton St., Germantown, Philadelphia, Pa.

McLANAHAN, GEORGE WILLIAM, 1601 21st St., Washington, D. C.

McLAUGHLIN, ANDREW CUNNINGHAM, A. M., LL. B., Professor of History, University of Chicago, Chicago, Ill.

MACLEISH, ANDREW, Glencoe, Ill.

McLENDON, SAMUEL GUYTON, B. L., Thomasville, Ga.

McMAHON, EDWARD, 708 State St., Madison, Wis. (Pacific Coast Branch.)

McMASTER, JOHN BACH, A. M., Ph. D., Litt. D., LL. D., Professor University of Pennsylvania, Philadelphia, Pa.

McMILLAN, WILLIAM CHARLES, A. B., Detroit, Mich.

McNAIR, FRED. WALTER, Houghton, Mich.

McNEAL, EDGAR HOLMES, Ph. D., Ohio State University, Columbus, Ohio.

McPHERSON, JOHN HANSON THOMAS, Ph. D., Professor University of Georgia, Athens, Ga.

MACVEAGH, FRANKLIN, LL. B., cor. Lake St. and Wabash Ave., Chicago, Ill.

*MACVEAGH, HON. WAYNE, LL. D., Brookfield Farm, Bryn Mawr, Pa.
MACY, JESSE, A. M., LL. D., Professor Iowa College, Grinnell, Iowa.
MACY, WILLIAM AUSTIN, M. D., Kings Park, Long Island, N. Y.
MADDUX, MRS. PARKER SIMMONS, 3586 California St., San Francisco, Cal.
MADEIRA, MISS LUCY, 1326 19th St., Washington, D. C.
MAGOUN, MISS ALICE NEAL, 4 N. Prospect St., Amherst, Mass.
MAHAN, ALFRED THAYER, D. C. L., LL. D., " Slumberside," Quogue, Long Island, New York.
MAHONEY, JAMES, A. B., Hotel Nottingham, Boston, Mass.
MAINE STATE LIBRARY, Augusta, Me.
MAITLAND, HON. ALEXANDER, Negaunee, Mich.
MALTBY, MISS MARTHA J., Central High School, 155 Lexington Ave., Columbus, Ohio.
MANIGAULT, DANIEL ELLIOTT HUGER, Socorro, Tex. (Pacific Coast Branch.)
MANN, CHARLES WESLEY, Lewis Institute, Chicago, Ill.
MANNHARDT, EMIL, 401 Schiller Building, Chicago, Ill.
MANNING, WILLIAM RAY, Ph. D., Purdue University, 312 Fowler Ave., Lafayette, Ind.
MANNING, WILLIAM WAYLAND, Room 6, 68 Devonshire St., Boston, Mass.
MANSFIELD, BURTON, ESQ., 436 Prospect St., New Haven, Conn.
MANTEL, CHARLES, Library of Congress, Washington, D. C.
MARGESSON, MISS HELEN PEARSON, A. B., 100 Melville Ave., Dorchester, Mass.
MARION, MAY PATTERSON (MRS. A. M.), B. S., Rural Route 1, Canonsburg, Pa.
MARKHAM, GEORGE DICKSON, A. B., LL. B., 4961 Berlin Ave., St. Louis, Mo.
MARLOW, MISS CORA E., B. A., 909 4th St., S. E., Minneopolis, Minn.
MARLOW, MISS KATHERINE K., Dorchester High School, Boston, Mass.
MARQUIS, MARY LEE, Albert Lea College for Women, Albert Lea, Minn.
MARSH, FRANK, Morristown, N. J.
MARSH, FRANK BURR, Assistant University of Michigan, 1112 Washtenaw Ave., Ann Arbor, Mich.
MARSH, MISS HARRIETTE P., Ph. B., 89 Whalley Ave., New Haven, Conn.
MARSH, HOWARD F., Wellsboro, Pa.
MARSTON, OLIVER JONES, A. M., Professor Ripon College, Ripon, Wis.
MARTIN, MISS ANNA H., A. M., Nevada State University, Reno, Nev.
MARTIN, HARRY WHEELER, 721 West Galena St., Butte, Mont.
MARTZOLFF, CLEMENT LUTHER, New Lexington, Ohio.
MARVIN, GEORGE T., Groton School, Groton, Mass.

MARYLAND HISTORICAL SOCIETY, 300 St. Paul St., Baltimore, Md.

MASON, VROMAN, care Chynoweth and Mason, Madison, Wis.

MASON, WILLIAM L., De Witt Clinton High School, New York, N. Y.

MASSACHUSETTS INSTITUTE OF TECHNOLOGY, Boston, Mass.

MATHENY, F. E., Casper, Wyo.

MATHER, J. BRUCE, Ph. D., D. D., History and Literature in North Side High School, 2939 Grove St., Denver, Colo.

MATHER, SAMUEL, Western Reserve Building, Cleveland, Ohio.

MATHEWS, MRS. LOIS KIMBALL, Vassar College, Poughkeepsie, N. Y.

MATHEWS, SHAILER, A. M., D. D., Professor University of Chicago, Chicago, Ill.

MATTESON, DAVID MAYDOLE, A. M., 1727 Cambridge St., Cambridge, Mass.

MATTESON, MISS FLORENCE M., 65 Ford Ave., Oneonta, N. Y.

MATTESON, GEORGE W. R., Providence, R. I.

MATTHEWS, ALBERT, A. B., Hotel Oxford, Boston, Mass.

MAY, MAX B., A. M., 32 Atlas Bank Building, Cincinnati, Ohio.

MAYBORN, MRS. MARY J., Emeryville, Cal.

MAYNARD, ARCHIBALD B., A. B., Professor University of South Dakota, Vermillion, S. Dak.

MAYNARD, COLTON, Cheshire, Conn.

MAYNARD, WILLIAM HALE, D. D., Professor Colgate University, Hamilton, N. Y.

MAYO, REV. ARMORY DWIGHT, A. M., LL. D., Bureau of Education, Washington, D. C.

MEAD, EDWIN DOAK, 20 Beacon St., Boston, Mass.

MEAD, NELSON P., A. M., Jerome Ave. and 174th St., New York, N. Y.

MEADVILLE THEOLOGICAL SCHOOL LIBRARY, Meadville, Pa.

MEANS, MRS. CELINA E., care Moore & Thomson, Columbia, S. C.

MEANY, EDMOND S., University Station, Seattle, Wash. (Pacific Coast Branch.)

MECHEM, FLOYD RUSSELL, A. M., Professor University of Chicago, 5714 Woodlawn Ave., Chicago, Ill.

MEEK, CHARLES S., Superintendent Public Schools, Elwood, Ind.

MEESE, WILLIAM A., Moline, Ill.

MEIGS, WILLIAM M., 841 Drexel Building, S. E. Corner 5th and Chestnut Sts., Philadelphia, Pa.

MELLBY, PROFESSOR C. A., Ph. D., 700 Orchard St., Northfield, Minn.

MELLEN, FRANK LOUIS, 5 Lagrange St., Worcester, Mass.

MELODY, MISS GENEVIEVE, Department of History, Chicago Normal School, 2964 Prairie Ave., Chicago, Ill.

MELTON, GEORGE LANE, Ph. B., University of Chicago, Chicago, Ill.

MENTZ, MISS DORA M., Marysville, Yuba• Co., Cal. (Pacific Coast Branch.)

MERCANTILE LIBRARY, Astor Place, New York, N. Y.

MERCUR, RODNEY AUGUSTUS, Towanda, Pa.

MERRIAM, CHARLES EDWARD, Ph. D., University of Chicago, Chicago, Ill.

MERRIAM, WILLIAM NELSON, Duluth, Minn.

MERRICK, GEORGE P., 100 Washington St., Chicago, Ill.

MERRILL, CHARLES AMOS, A. M., LL. B., Rooms 4 and 5, Worcester Five Cents Savings Bank Building, Worcester, Mass.

MERRIMAN, REV. DANIEL, D. D., 8 Institute Road, Worcester, Mass.

MERRIMAN, EDWARD DE WITT, A. M., Rural Free Delivery, Coventry, Conn.

MERRIMAN, HON. GEORGE WEAVER, B. L., Hartford, Van Buren Co., Mich.

MERRIMAN, ROGER BIGELOW, B. Litt. (Oxon), Ph. D., 26 Quincy St., Cambridge, Mass.

MERRITT, MRS. CORA A., 698 Sycamore St., Oakland, Cal. (Pacific Coast Branch.)

MERTEN, FREDERICK HENRY, B. A., Greeley, Colo.

MERTZ, JOHN WILLIAM, Fairfield Centre, Ind.

MESSMER, SEBASTIAN GEBHARD, D. D., D. C. L., Bishop of Green Bay, 2224 Chestnut St., Milwaukee, Wis.

MESSMORE, MISS ELIZABETH, 339 York St., Salt Lake City, Utah.

MICHIGAN STATE NORMAL COLLEGE, Ypsilanti, Mich.

MIKKELSEN, MICHAEL ANDREW, Ph. D., 54 Grove St., Tarrytown, N. Y.

MILITARY ORDER OF LOYAL LEGION OF THE UNITED STATES, Headquarters Commandery of the State of Illinois, 320 Ashland Block, Chicago, Ill.

MILLER, BERTHA A., High School, 310 W. Washington St., Paris, Ill.

MILLER, CHARLES F., Nappanee, Ind.

MILLER, HON. CHARLES ROLLIN, LL. B., M. S., Adrian, Mich.

MILLER, CHARLES TYLER, Ph. B., care Ray Chemical Co., Detroit, Mich.

MILLER, EDGAR G., 646 Equitable Building, Baltimore, Md.

MILLER, ELMER ISAIAH, A. M., State Normal School, Chico, Cal. (Pacific Coast Branch.)

MILLER, MARINDA WINSOR, 1105 Millar Ave., Chicago, Ill.

MILLER, THOMAS CONDIT, A. M., State Superintendent of Schools, Charleston, W. Va.

MILLS, LT. COL., R. E., Royal Engineer's Office, Tersly, Channel Islands.

MIMS, STEWART LEA, 716 West Divinity Hall, Yale University, New Haven, Conn.

MILWAUKEE PUBLIC LIBRARY, Milwaukee, Wis.

MINER, WILLIAM HARVEY, care The Burrows Brothers,. Cleveland, Ohio.

MINNEAPOLIS ATHENAEUM, Minneapolis, Minn.

MITCHELL, BENJAMIN WIESTLING, Ph. D., Professor Central High School, Philadelphia, Pa.

MITCHELL, CHARLES ANDREWS, A. B., Asheville·School, Asheville, N. C.

MITCHELL, CLARE JANE, 32 West Mechanic St., Shelbyville, Ind.

MITCHELL, EDWIN KNOX, D. D., Professor Hartford Theological Seminary, Hartford, Conn.

MITCHELL, JAMES ENNIS, A. M., Professor Alma College, Alma, Mich.

MITCHELL, KIRKWOOD, 303 West Grace St., Richmond, Va.

MITCHELL, SAMUEL CHILES, Ph. D., Richmond College, Richmond, Va.

MITCHELL, WILLIAM HUGH, University School, Cleveland, Ohio.

MONAGHAN, JAMES CHARLES, 1335 F St., Washington, D. C.

MONCRIEF, JOHN WILDMAN, A. M., D. D., Professor University of Chicago, Chicago, Ill.

MONROE, PAUL, Ph. D., Teachers' College, Columbia University, New York, N. Y.

MONTGOMERY, HON. M. A., LL. B., Oxford, Miss.

MONTGOMERY, THOMAS LYNCH, A. B., State Library, Harrisburg, Pa.

MONTCLAIR FREE PUBLIC LIBRARY, Montclair, N. J.

MOORE, ANNA L., Framingham, Mass.

MOORE, CHARLES, Ph. D., 99 Warren St., Brookline, Mass.

MOORE, EDITH R., B. A., 672 Summit Ave., St. Paul, Minn.

MOORE, ERNEST CARROLL, Professor in University of California, 1227 Washington St., San Francisco, Cal. (Pacific Coast Branch.)

MOORE, FREDERICK WIGHTMAN, Ph. D., Professor Vanderbilt University, Nashville, Tenn.

MOORE, HON. JOHN BASSETT, LL. D., Columbia University, New York. ‘

*MOORE, JOSEPH, JR., A. M., F. R. G. S., 1821 Walnut St., Philadelphia, Pa.

MOORE, JOSEPH E., Thomaston, Me.

MOORE, JOSEPH R. H., A. B., 26 Whittier St., Cambridge, Mass.

MOORE, HON. R. WALTON, Fairfax, Va.

MORAN, THOMAS FRANCIS, Ph. D., Professor Purdue University, Lafayette, Ind.

MOREHEAD, CHARLES R., President State National Bank, El Paso, Texas.

MOREHEAD, JOSEPH MOTLEY, President Guilford Battle Ground Co., Greensboro, N. C.

MOREHOUSE, LINDEN HUSTED, Editor *The Young Churchman*, 412 Milwaukee St.. Milwaukee, Wis.

MOLERA, EUSEBIUS J., 2025 Sacramento St., San Francisco, Cal. (Pacific Coast Branch.)

MOREY, WILLIAM CAREY, Ph. D., D. C. L., Professor University of Rochester, Rochester, N. Y.

MORGAN, EDWIN VERNON, A. B., Department of State, Washington, D. C.

MORGAN, FORREST, M. A., 227 Sigourney St., Hartford, Conn.

MORGAN, FREDERIC GRINNELL, A. B., Vice Consul General, Cairo, Egypt.

MORRILL, MISS JENNY H., P. O. Box 409, Daytona, Fla.

MORRIS, CHARLES MARCIUS, A. B., LL. B., Rooms 503-5, Colby-Abbot Building, Milwaukee, Wis.

MORRIS, EDWARD, 4500 Michigan Ave., Chicago, Ill.

MORRIS, HENRY CRITTENDEN, A. M., 4442 Grand Boulevard, Chicago, Ill.

MORRIS, HOWARD, Wisconsin Central Railroad, Milwaukee, Wis.

MORRIS, MISS MARGARET S., 1904 Mount Royal Terrace, Baltimore, Md.

MORRIS, SEYMOUR, Governor Society of Colonial Wars, Room 901 Merchants' Loan and Trust Building, 135 Adams St., Chicago, Ill.

MORRIS, WILLIAM ALFRED, A. B., Harvard University, Cambridge, Mass.

MORRISON, A. F., A. B., LL. B., Crocker Building, San Francisco, Cal. (Pacific Coast Branch.)

MORSE, ANSON ELY, M. A., Amherst, Mass.

MORSE, ANSON DANIEL, LL. D., Professor Amherst College, Amherst, Mass.

MORSE, EDWARD L., C., 9009 Escanaba Ave., Chicago, Ill.

MORSE, HORACE HENRY, A. M., 27 Hudson St., Somerville, Mass.

MORSE, JOHN TORREY, JR., A. B., 16 Fairchild St., Boston, Mass.

MORTON, MRS. JENNIE C., Secretary and Treasurer, Kentucky State Historical Society, Frankfort, Ky.

MOSBY, MRS. FANNIE JAMES, Professor of History Industrial Institute and College, 716 N. 2d Ave., Columbus, Miss.

MOSENTHAL, PHILIP JAMES, M. S., 46 Cedar St., New York, N. Y.

MOSES, BERNARD, Ph. D., LL. D., University of California, Berkeley, Cal. (Pacific Coast Branch.)

MOSES, MABELLE L., 19 Putnam St., West Newton, Mass.

MOSS, CLAUDE RUSSELL, Baguio, Benguet, P. I.

MOULTON, MISS A. FLORENCE, Holman School, 2204 Walnut St., Philadelphia, Pa.

MOULTON, HON. AUGUSTUS F,. A. M., 98 Exchange St., Portland, Me.

MOUNT HOLYOKE COLLEGE, South Hadley, Mass.

MOUNT, MISS LUCY C., Sonora, Tuolumne Co., Cal. (Pacific Coast Branch.)

MOWRY, WILLIAM AUGUSTUS, A. M., Ph. D., LL. D., 17 Riverside Square, Hyde Park, Mass.

MULLAY, MISS ANNA, 5844 Rosalie Court, Chicago, Ill.

MÜLLER, LOUIS, 304 Chamber of Commerce, Baltimore, Md.

MUNDY, EZEKIEL W., A. M., Litt. D., Public Library, Syracuse, N. Y.

MUNFORD, MISS ELIZABETH UNDERWOOD, 1208 Demonbreun St., Nashville, Tenn.

MUNRO, MISS ANNETTE G., Bristol, R. I.

MUNRO, DANA CARLETON, A. M., Professor University of Wisconsin, Madison, Wis.

MUNRO, WILFRED HAROLD, A. M., Professor Brown University, Providence, R. I.

MUNRO, WILLIAM BENNETT, LL. B., Ph. D., Assistant Professor of Government in Harvard University, 37 Dana Chambers, Cambridge, Mass.

MURPHY, MISS ELLEN JANE, Marion, S. C.

MURRAY, DANIEL M., Ellicott City, Md.

P. M. MUSSER PUBLIC LIBRARY, Muscatine, Iowa.

MUZZEY, DAVID S., 30 Lincoln Terrace, Yonkers, N. Y.

MYERS, ALBERT COOK, M. L., Moylan, Pa.

MYERS, PHILIP VAN NESS, L. H. D., College Hill, Ohio.

MYERS, WILLIAM STARR, Ph. D., 26 Bank St., Princeton, N. J.

MYRICK, MRS. MARIA L., 595 Johnson St., Portland, Ore. (Pacific Coast Branch.)

NASH, FRANCIS, Hillsboro, N. C.

NASH, LYMAN JUNIUS, Manitowoc, Wis.

NATH, B. D., Bengalore City, British India.

NAUGHTIN, REV. JOHN M., Madison, Wis.

NAUMAN, GEORGE P., M. S., Professor Northwestern College, Naperville, Ill.

NEAD, BENJAMIN MATTHIAS, A. B., Attorney at Law, Harrisburg, Pa.

NEESER, ROBERT W., A. B., University Club, Washington, D. C.

NEILSON, MISS NELLIE, Ph. D., Mount Holyoke College, South Hadley, Mass.

NELSON, HON. EDWARD DEANE, Ironwood, Mich.

NELSON, HENRY LOOMIS, L. H. D., Williams College, Williamstown, Mass.

NELSON, JAMES CARLTON, Teacher American History, Dubuque High School, 1073 Locust St., Dubuque, Iowa.

NELSON, PETER, A. B., 135 South Swan St., Albany, N. Y.

NELSON, WILLIAM, A. M., Corresponding Secretary New Jersey Historical Society, Paterson, N. J.

NEWARK FREE PUBLIC LIBRARY, Newark, N. J.

NEWBERRY LIBRARY, Chicago, Ill.

NEWELL, AARON, B. A., Cumberland, Wash.

NEWELL, JAMES BLAIR, Petaluma, Cal. (Pacific Coast Branch.)

NEWHALL, ALBERT HITCHINS, A. M., 19 East 41st St., New York, N. Y.

NEW HAMPSHIRE COLLEGE LIBRARY, Durham, N. H.

NEWMAN, ALBERT HENRY, D. D., LL. D., Baylor University, Waco, Tex.

NEWMAN, STEPHEN MORRELL, D. D., 10th and G Sts., N. W., Washington, D. C.

NEWTON, CHARLES BERTRAM, Lawrenceville School, Lawrenceville, N. J.

NEWTON, LEWIS WILLIAM, University of Texas, Austin, Tex.

NEWTON, SUSAN, Athens, Ga.

NEW YORK UNIVERSITY HISTORICAL SOCIETY, University Heights, New York, N. Y.

NICHOLS, WALTER HAMMOND, Boulder, Colo.

NIGHTINGALE, GEORGE C., Providence, R. I.

NISSENSEN, S. G., 108 West 124th St., New York, N. Y.

NOBLE, HENRY HARMON, Essex, N. Y.

NOBLE, JOHN, LL. D., Clerk Supreme Judicial Court of the Commonwealth ond Corresponding Secretary Colonial Society of Massachusetts, Court House, Boston, Mass.

NOBLE, JOHN, JR., A. B., LL. B., 66 Sparks St., Cambridge, Mass.

NOLAN, JOHN THOMAS, 1103 Jennings St., New York.

NORCROSS, FREDERICK F., 704 Marquette Building, Chicago, Ill.

NORCROSS, GEORGE, D. D., Pastor Second Presbyterian Church, Carlisle, Pa.

NORRIS, MISS ETHELDREDA LORD, B. A., Pd. M., 71 Atlantic St., Jersey City, N. J.

NORTHROP, AMANDA CAROLYN, 19 East 41st St., New York, N. Y.

NORTON, CHARLES ELIOT, LL. D., D. C. L., Professor Harvard University, Cambridge, Mass.

NORTON, DAVID Z., Cleveland, Ohio.

NORTON, MRS. HELEN BENDER, 4827 Lake Ave., Chicago, Ill.

NORTON, WILLIAM J., 26 East 48th St., New York, N. Y.

NORWICH UNIVERSITY LIBRARY, Northfield, Vt.

NORWOOD, J. NELSON, Alfred, N. Y.

NOTESTEIN, WALLACE, Lawrence, Kansas.

NOUVION, FERNAND G., Member de la Societe d'Histoire Moderne, Avenue du Roule 105, Neuilly sur Seine, France.

NOYES, DANIEL ROGERS, 366 Summit Ave., St. Paul, Minn.

NOYES, EDMUND S., Central High School, Washington, D. C.

NOYES, ELIZABETH BROWNING, M. L., 55 Franklin Ave., Oshkosh, Wis.

NOYES, JAMES ATKINS, A. B., 71 Sparks St., Cambridge, Mass.

OBERHOLTZER, ELLIS PAXSON, Ph. D., 1905 Tioga St., Philadelphia, Pa.

O'BRIEN, REV. FRANK A., A. M., LL. D., Kalamazoo, Mich.

O'BRIEN, MISS MABEL G., Merced, Cal. (Pacific Coast Branch.)

O'BRIEN, MICHAEL W., Detroit, Mich.

O'CALLAGHAN, REV. T., San Mateo, Cal.

OGG, FREDERIC AUSTIN, A. M., Harvard University, Cambridge, Mass.

OLESON, PETER, Ph. B., 1607 Hewitt Ave., St. Paul, Minn.

OLIN, JOHN M., A. M., 1 W. Main St., Madison, Wis.

OLMSTEAD, ALBERT TEN EYCK, A. B., A. M., Fellow of American School for Oriental Studies (Jerusalem, Syria), Ithaca, N. Y.

OLMSTEAD, WILLIAM BEACH, A. B., Head Master Pomfret School, Pomfret, Conn.

OMAHA PUBLIC LIBRARY, Omaha, Neb.

O'NEAL, MRS. M. L., 419 Ashbury St., San Francisco, Cal. (Pacific Coast Branch.)

ORBEGOSO, SENOR LUIS VARELA Y, Apartado Numero N. 26, Lima, Peru.

ORR, CHARLES, Librarian Case Library, Cleveland, Ohio.

ORR, MISS ELLA, Butte, Mont. (Pacific Coast Branch.)

ORTON, MRS. EDWARD, JR., The Normandie, Columbus, Ohio.

ORVIS, MISS JULIA SWIFT, A. B., Wellesley College, Wellesley, Mass.

OSBORN, HARTWELL, 1314 Asbury Ave., Evanston, Cook Co., Ill.

OSBORN, MARY GEORGE, A. M., Warren, R. I.

OSGOOD, HERBERT LEVI, Ph. D., Professor Columbia University, New York, N. Y.

OSGOOD, HOWARD LAWRENCE, Vice-President Historical Society, 804 Wilder Building, Rochester, N. Y.

OTIS, HON. EPHRAIM ALLEN, 13 Astor St., Chicago, Ill.

OTIS, JOSEPH E., President Western Trust and Savings Bank, Chicago, Ill.

OTT, EDWIN, 41 Perkins Hall, Harvard University, Cambridge, Mass.

OVINGTON, MARY WHITE, Hotel St. George, Brooklyn, N. Y.

OWEN, THOMAS MCADORY, A. M., LL. D., Director of the Department of Archives and History of the State of Alabama, Montgomery, Ala.

*PACK, HON. GEORGE WILLIS, Asheville, N. C.

PADDOCK, MISS HELEN LAURA, B. A., Waterville, N. Y.

PAGE, EDWARD CARLTON, A. B., Professor Northern Illinois State Normal School, De Kalb, Ill.

PAGE, ROLPH BARLOW, 537 W. 123rd St., New York, N. Y.

PAGE, THOMAS NELSON, Litt. D., LL. D., 1759 R St., Washington, D. C.

PAGE, THOMAS WALKER, Ph. D., University of Virginia, Charlottesville, Va. (Pacific Coast Branch.)

PAGE, WALTER H., 133–137 E. 16th St., New York, N. Y.

PAHLOW, EDWIN WILLIAM, M. A., 83 Prospect St., Reading, Mass.

PAINE, FREDERIC H., A. M., 285 Quincy St., Brooklyn, N. Y.

PAINE, NATHANIEL, A. M., Treasurer American Antiquarian Society, Worcester, Mass.

PALMER, CHARLES RAY, D. D., 562 Whitney Ave., New Haven, Conn.

PALMER, GEORGE M., Milaca Public School, Milaca, Minn.

PALMER, MISS HERRIOTT CLARE, Ph. M., 505 West 124th St., New York, N. Y.

PALTSITS, VICTOR HUGO, New York Public Library (Lenox Building), 5th Ave. and 70th St., New York, N. Y.

PARHAM, R. H., Principal of Kramer School, 903 Scott St., Little Rock, Ark.

PARK, FRED W., Station A., Lincoln, Neb.

PARK, JAMES, Public Accountant, Exchange Court Bldg., 52 Broadway, New York, N. Y.

PARKER, BARTON L., B. L., LL. B., Green Bay, Wis.

PARKER, FRANCIS HUBERT, A. B., LL. B., 902 Main St., Hartford, Conn.

PARKER, MISS FLORA E., 504 Grand River Ave., Detroit, Mich.

PARKER, MISS LAURA M., Instructor in History, Baylor University, Waco, Tex.

PARKER, MISS LELAH MARIE, B. L., A. M., Cor. 10th St. and 4th Ave., Durango, Col. (Pacific Coast Branch.)

PARKER, LAURENCE HOUGHTON, West Hartford, Conn.

PARKER, HON. LEONARD FLETCHER, D. D., Professor Emeritus Iowa College, Grinnell, Iowa.

PARKER, MISS MARILLA ZEROYDA, Ph. B., Tecaher of History, Phillips High School, 5624 Ellis Ave., Chicago, Ill.

PARKER, ROBERT B., 67 Manning St., Providence, R. I.

PARKER, WALTER SCOTT, B. S., Reading, Mass.

PARKHURST, MISS EDITH ADELAIDE, 22 Hiland Ave., Somerville, Mass.

PARSONS, MISS ALICE KNIGHT, Principal Girls' Collegiate School, Los Angeles, Cal. (Pacific Coast Branch.)

PARSONS, ARTHUR JEFFREY, Chief of Division of Prints, Library of Congress, Washington, D. C.

PARSONS, EBEN BURT, A. M., D. D., Williams College, Williamstown, Mass.

PATTERSON, CHARLES FLORENCE, Ph. B., Superintendent of Schools, Tipton, Ind.

PATTERSON, DAVID L., JR., 621 Francis St., Madison, Wis.

PATTERSON, MRS. GEORGE W., President Patterson Library, West-field, N. Y.

*PATTERSON, JAMES WILSON, A. M., F. R. G. S., 14 Mt. Vernon Place, East, Baltimore, Md.

PATTON, HON. JOHN, JR., A. B., Grand Rapids, Mich.

PATRICK, LEWIS SEAMAN, Marinette, Wis.

PAULLIN, CHARLES OSCAR, Ph. D., 109 2nd St. S. E., Washington, D. C.

PAXSON, FREDERIC LOGAN, Ph. D., University of Colorado, Boulder, Colo.

PEARSON, GEORGE EDWARD, A. M., Assistant in History Tufts College, 325 Highland Ave., West Somerville, Mass.

PEARSON, HENRY GREENLEAF, Massachusetts Institute of Technology, Boston, Mass.

PEASE, HENRY, A. M., Superintendent of Schools, Titusville, Pa.

PEASE, WILLIAM A., 2321 No. 42nd Court, Chicago, Ill.

PECK, A. L., Gloversville, N. Y.

PECK, MRS. MARIA PURDY, 723 Brady St., Davenport, Iowa.

PECK, MISS MARIA STORRS, A. M., 106 George St., Providence, R. I.

PECK, PAUL F., Ph. D., Iowa College, Grinnell, Iowa.

PEEPLES, ROBERT HAL, Peeples School, Franklin, Tenn.

PEIRCE, PAUL SKEELS, Ph. D., Assistant Professor Iowa State College, Ames, Iowa.

PEIRSON, CHARLES LAWRENCE, S. B., A. M., 191 Commonwealth Ave., Boston, Mass.

PELLEW, HENRY E., 1637 Massachusetts Ave. N. W., Washington, D. C.

PENROSE, STEPHEN BEASLEY LINNARD, 41 College Ave., Walla Walla, Wash. (Pacific Coast Branch.)

PERDUE, MISS ROSA M., Plymouth, Wis.

PERELES, HON. JAMES M., LL. B., City Hall Square, Milwaukee, Wis.

PERELES, THOMAS JEFFERSON, LL. B., City Hall Square, Milwaukee, Wis.

PERKINS, CLARENCE, A. M., 24 Irving St., Cambridge, Mass.

PERKINS, HON. EDWIN RUTHVEN, A. B., LL. D., 10 Commercial Bank Building, Cleveland, Ohio.

PERKINS, HON. JAMES BRECK, LL. D., Wilder Building, Rochester, N. Y.

PERKINS, JAMES LAMONT, 1201 Chestnut St., Philadelphia, Pa.

PERKINS, MOSES BRADSTREET, 20 Montrose St., Roxbury, Mass.

PERKINS, R. W., M. A., Ph. D., President of Leland University, New Orleans, La.

PERRIN, BERNADOTTE, LL. D., Professor Yale University, New Haven, Conn.

PERRIN, JOHN WILLIAM, Ph. D., Librarian, Case Library, Cleveland, Ohio.

PERRY, HARLOW S., Ph. D., Dartmouth College, Hanover, N. H.

PERRY, ARTHUR, A. B., 60 State St., Boston, Mass.

PERRY, MRS. MARY N., 920 Madison Ave., Baltimore, Md.

PERSON, HARLOW S., Ph. D., Dartmouth College, Hanover, N. H.

PESKIND, ARNOLD, M. D., 1377 Willson Ave., Cleveland, Ohio.

PETER WHITE PUBLIC LIBRARY, Marquette, Mich.

PETERSON, CONRAD ALBIN, Box 311, Duquesne, Pa.

PETERSON, CYRUS ASBURY, M. D., President Missouri Historical Society, 8 Shaw Place, St. Louis, Mo.

PETRIE, DR. GEORGE, Alabama Polytechnic Institute, Auburn, Ala.

PETTEGREW, DAVID LYMAN, P. O. Box 75, Worcester, Mass.

PETTIBONE, JOHN, Ph. B., New Milford, Conn.

PETTINGILL, TALLAHATCLIN, Stanford University, Cal. (Pacific Coast Branch.)

PFINGST, MRS. FLORENCE, Watsonville, Cal.

PHAYRE, JOHN F., 105 West 121st St., New York, N. Y.

PHELAN, HON. JAMES D., 301 Phelan Building, San Francisco, Cal. (Pacific Coast Branch.)

PHELAN, MISS MARY L., S. W. Valencia and 17th Sts., San Francisco Cal. (Pacific Coast Branch.)

PHELPS, PETER W., Marquette, Mich.

PHILBRICK, FRANCIS SAMUEL, Ph. D., 1023 H St., Lincoln, Neb.

PHILLIPS, ULRICH BONNELL, A. M., Ph. D., Instructor in History, University of Wisconsin, Madison, Wis.

PIERCE, HENRY CLAY, Waldorf-Astoria, New York, N. Y.

PIERCE, HOWARD H., 2442 Hoagland Ave., Fort Wayne, Ind.

PILLOT, MRS. MARY AUGUSTA, San Jose High School, 85 S. 11th St., San Jose, Cal. (Pacific Coast Branch.)

PILLSBURY, WILLIAM LOW, A. M., University of Illinois, Urbana, Ill.

PIPES, JOHN M., Eugene, Ore. (Pacific Coast Branch.)

PITMAN, FRANK WESLEY, 119 Gilbert Ave., New Haven, Conn.

PITTS, THOMAS, Detroit, Mich.

PLANK, LOUIS, 7 Seventh Ave., Richmond District, San Francisco, Cal. (Pacific Coast Branch.)

PLATNER, SAMUEL BALL, Ph. D., Adelbert College, Cleveland, Ohio.

PLATNER, JOHN WINTHROP, A. M., D. D., Professor Andover Theological Seminary, Andover, Mass.

PLUM, HARRY GRANT, M. A., Ph. D., Professor of European History, State University of Iowa, Iowa City, Iowa.

PLUMB, ROBERT E., 931 Jefferson Ave., Detroit, Mich.

PLYMPTON, GILBERT MOTIER, LL. B., 27 William St., New York.

POMONA COLLEGE LIBRARY, Claremont, Cal.

POND, ASHLEY, Detroit, Mich.

POPE, COL. ALBERT AUGUSTUS, 221 Columbus Ave., Boston, Mass.

*POPE, ALFRED A., M. A., Farmington, Conn.

PORRITT, EDWARD, 63 Tremont St., Hartford, Conn.

PORTER, GEORGE HENRY, 175 West 10th Ave., Columbus, Ohio.

PORTER, MARY M., Chair of History and Civics, St. Joseph High School, 412 N. 8th St., St. Joseph, Mo.

POST, ABRAM S., 81 and 83 Fulton St., New York, N. Y.

POTTER, EDWIN A., N. Y. Life Building, Chicago, Ill.

POTTER, EDWIN O., Eugene, Ore. (Pacific Coast Branch.)

POTTER, EMERY DAVIS, LL. B., Toledo, Ohio.

POTTER, GEORGE SABINE, A. B., Noble and Greenough's Classical School, 100 Beacon St., Boston, Mass.

POTTER, HENRY CAMP, JR., care State Savings Bank, Detroit, Mich.

POWELL, BURT EARDLY, Ph. D., Wilmette, Ill.

POWERS, J. N., Superintendent of City Graded Schools, West Point, Miss.

POWERS, MRS. LAURA BRIDE, 1098 Post St., San Francisco, Cal. (Pacific Coast Branch.)

PRAG, MRS. MARY, Girls' High School, San Francisco, Cal. (Pacific Coast Branch.)

PRATT, DANIEL, Prattville, Ala.

PRATT INSTITUTE FREE LIBRARY, Brooklyn, N. Y.

*PRENTICE, E. PARMALEE, 35 Wall St., New York, N. Y.

PRENTICE, F. W., Eugene, Ore. (Pacific Coast Branch.)

PRESTON, MISS HELEN GERTRUDE, Ph. D., 2312 Poplar St., Philadelphia, Pa.

*PRESTON, HOWARD WILLIS, A. M., Providence, R. I.

PRICE, RALPH RAY, A. B., A. M., Professor of History and Economics, State Agricultural College, 826 Houston St., Manhattan, Kan.

PRICE, WILLIAM WIGHTMAN, A. M., Agassiz Hall, Alta, Placer Co., Cal. (Pacific Coast Branch.)

PRINCE, BENJAMIN FRANKLIN, Ph. D., Professor Wittenberg College, Springfield, Ohio.

PRINCE, REV. WALTER FRANKLIN, B. D., Ph. D.,16 South Elliott Place, Brooklyn, N. Y.

PROVIDENCE ATHENÆUM, Providence, R. I.

PRUSSING, EUGENE E., Room 567 The Rookery, Chicago, Ill.

PUBLIC LIBRARY, Cazenovia, N. Y.

PUBLIC LIBRARY, Greenfield, Mass.

PUBLIC LIBRARY OF BROOKLINE, Brookline, Mass.

PUBLIC LIBRARY OF THE DISTRICT OF COLUMBIA, Washington, D. C.

PUBLIC LIBRARY, Haverhill, Mass.

PUBLIC LIBRARY, Rockford, Ill.

PUBLIC LIBRARY, Salem, Mass.

PUCHNER, RUDOLPH, New Holstein, Wis.

PUGSLEY, MISS ANNA M., Dean of Wilson College, Chambersburg, Pa.

PUIG, MISS LOUISE M., 868 Sterling Place, Brooklyn, N. Y.

PURMORT, MRS. HENRY CLAY, 3430 Prairie Ave., Chicago, Ill.

PUSEY, DR. WILLIAM ALLEN, Evanston, Ill.

PUTNAM, MISS BERTHA HAVEN, 335 W. 86th St., New York, N. Y.

PUTNAM, FREDERIC WARD, A. M., S. D., Professor Harvard University, Cambridge, Mass.; also University of California, Berkeley, Cal.

PUTNAM, HARRINGTON, 404 Washington Ave., Brooklyn, N. Y.

PUTNAM, HERBERT, Litt. D., LL. D., Librarian of Congress, Library of Congress, Washington, D. C.

PUTNAM, HERBERT S., County Superintendent, Towanda, Pa.

PUTNAM, JAMES WILLIAM, A. M., University of Missouri, Columbus, Mo.

PUTNAM, MARY BURNHAM, Ph. B., B. Pd., State Normal College, Ypsilanti, Mich.

PUTNAM, MISS RUTH, B. Lit., 27 W. 23rd St., New York.

PYNE, MOSES TAYLOR, A. M., L. H. D., Drumthwacket, Princeton, N. J.

QUAIFE, MILO MILTON, Ph. B., Nashua, Iowa.

QUINBY, MISS MARIA ANTOINETTE, President Woman's Auxiliary New Jersey State Historical Society, Newark, N. J.

RADCLIFFE COLLEGE LIBRARY, Cambridge, Mass.

RADEBAUGH, WILLIAM, Chicago Normal School, 6537 Perry Ave., Chicago, Ill.

RAGSDALE, MRS. LENA MOSELEY, Madison St., Clarksville, Tenn.

RAMAGE, BURR JAMES, Ph. D., Department of Commerce and Labor, Bureau of Corporations, Washington, D. C.

RAMMELKAMP, CHARLES HENRY, Ph. D., Illinois College, Jacksonville, Ill.

RAMSDELL, CHARLES W., University of Texas, Austin, Tex.

RAMSAY WILLIAM M., Westover, Va.

RANCK, SAMUEL HAVERSTICK, Librarian Public Library, Grand Rapids, Mich.

RAND, BENJAMIN, Ph. D., Harvard University, Cambridge, Mass.

RAND, CHARLES F., 71 Broadway, New York.

RANDALL, HON. EMILIUS OVIATT, LL. M., Secretary Ohio State Archæological and Historical Society, Columbus, O.

RANDOLPH, BEVERLY S., Berkeley Springs, West Va.

RANDOLPH-MACON, COLLEGE, Ashland, Va.

RANGER, HON. WALTER EUGENE, A. M., 267 Gano St., Providence, R. I.

RANKIN, THOMAS ERNEST, A. M., 1713 South University Ave., Ann Arbor, Mich.

RAPER, CHARLES LEE, Ph. D., Professor of Economics, University of North Carolina, Chapel Hill, N. C.

RATHER, ETHEL J., 131 Howe St., New Haven, Conn.

RAWLE, FRANCIS, A. M., LL. B., 328 Chestnut St., Philadelphia, Pa.

RAWLE, WILLIAM BROOKE, A. M., A Vice-President, Hist. Soc. of Penna., 211 S. Sixth St., Philadelphia, Pa.

RAWLES, WILLIAM, A. M., Ph. D., Professor Indiana State University, Bloomington, Ind.

RAY, GEORGE RANKIN, B. A., Beloit College, Beloit, Wis.

RAY, PERLEY ORMAN, A. M., Professor of History and Political Science, Pennsylvania State College, State College, Pa.

RAYMOND, SAMUEL ATWATER, Western Reserve Bldg., Cleveland, Ohio.

READ, CONYERS, 211 Chestnut St., Philadelphia, Pa.

READ, WILLIAM, 107 Washington St., Boston, Mass.

READER, FRANCIS S., Beaver Valley News, New Brighton, Pa.

REED, ANNA Y. (Mrs. J. A.), Ph. D., 523 West 121st St., New York, N. Y.

REED, CHARLES L., Teacher of History in Mechanic Arts High School, Boston, Mass., 38 Riverview Road, Brighton, Mass.

REED, JOSEPH, A. B., Box 429, Glenwood, Colo.

REED, MISS LOIS A., care Carl Cutler, 528 West 123rd St., New York, N. Y.

REED, REV. WILLARD, 26 Walker St., Cambridge, Mass.

REESE, LOUIS A., 32 East 28th St., New York, N. Y.

REEVES, JESSE SIDDALL, Ph. D., Richmond, Ind.

REEVES, REV. THOMAS ROSSER, B. A., M. E. Church South, Franklin, Va.

REID, MISS EMILY J., A. B., Principal Ruth Hargrove Seminary, Key West, Fla.

REID, WILLIAM MAX, ex-President Board of Trade, Cor. Secy. Montgomery County Historical Society, 58 Market St., Amsterdam, N. Y.

REILEY, ALAN C., 327 Broadway, New York, N. Y.

REINSCH, PAUL S., Ph. D., Professor University of Wisconsin, Madison, Wis.

REW, IRWIN, 1106 Oak Ave., Evanston, Ill.

REX, PERCIVAL TAYLOR, 421 South 43d St., Philadelphia, Pa.

REYNOLDS, DORRANCE, 92 South River St., Wilkes-Barre, Pa.

REYNOLDS, J. H., A. M., Professor University of Arkansas, Fayetteville, Ark.

REYNOLDS, MARION FRED, P. O. Box 210, Modesto, Cal. (Pacific Coast Branch.)

REYNOLDS, WILLIAM, A. M., Meadville, Pa.

RHODES, HON. BRADFORD, 76 William St., New York, N. Y.

RHODES, CHARLES HARKER, Hennessey, Okla.

*RHODES JAMES FORD, LL. D., Litt. D., 392 Beacon St., Boston, Mass.

RICE, MISS EMILY J., Ph. B., School of Education, University of Chicago, Chicago, Ill.

RICE, HARRY E., B. Pd., Instructor, Ferris Institute, Big Rapids, Mich.

RICE, RICHARD A., Professor Williams College, Williamstown, Mass.

RICE, WILLIAM CHAUNCEY, A. B., A. M., 53 Newtonville Ave., Newton, Mass.

RICHARDS, L. D., Fremont, Neb.

RICHARDS, WILLIAM H., 420 Fifth St., N. W., Washington, D. C.

RICHARDSON, ALBERT LEVIN, President The Public Records Commission of Maryland, 817 N. Charles St., Baltimore, Md.

RICHARDSON, CHARLES FRANCIS, Ph. D., Professor of English, Dartmouth College, Hanover, N. H.

RICHARDSON, ERNÉST CUSHING, Ph. D., Princeton, N. J.

RICHARDSON, MRS. HESTER DORSEY (Mrs. A. L.), 817 North Charles St. Baltimore, Md.

RICHARDSON, LILLIE, Home Institute, 1440 Camp St., New Orleans, La.

RICHARDSON, OLIVER HUNTINGTON, Ph. D., Professor Yale University, 284 Orange St., New Haven, Conn.

RICHARDSON, ROBERT KIMBALL, A. M., Ph. D., Beloit, Wis.

RICHARDSON, W. H., Mineral City, Ohio.

RICHMOND, HENRY A., Corner Delaware Ave. and Tupper St., Buffalo, N. Y.

RIDER, WILLIAM LESLIE, A. B.,A. M., 1020 N. Oregon St., El Paso, Tex.

RIESS, JOHN R., Sheboygan, Wis.

RIGGS, JAMES FORSYTH, D. D., 430 William St., East Orange, N. J.

RIGHTMIRE, GEORGE W., 44 W. Broad St., Columbus, Ohio.

RILEY, REV. B. F., Houston, Texas.

RILEY, FRANKLIN LAFAYETTE, A. M., Ph. D., Professor University of Mississippi, University, Miss.

RILEY, SAMUEL GAYLE, Jacksonville, Tenn.

RIPTON, BENJAMIN HENRY, Ph. D., LL. D., Professor Union College, Schenectady, N. Y.

RISLEY, PROFESSOR A. W., Colgate University, Hamilton, N. Y.

ROBERTS, AGNES I., High School, Bayfield, Wis.

ROBERTS, FRANK H. H., A. M., Ph. D., University Park, Colo. (Pacific Coast Branch.)

ROBERTS, JOHATHAN W., Morris Plains, N. J.

ROBERTSON, JAMES A., Historical Library, Madison, Wis.

ROBERTSON, JAMES ROOD, A. M., Professor Pacific University, Forest Grove, Oregon. (Pacifi Coast Branch.)

ROBERTSON, THOMAS BROWN, Eastville, Va.

ROBERTSON, WILLIAM SPENCE, Ph. D., 24 Adelbert Hall, Cleveland, O.

ROBINS, GEORGE DOUGLAS, A. B., LL. B., The High School, Pottstown, Pa.

ROBINSON, ALBERT JACKSON, Hubbard, Texas.

ROBINSON, CHALFANT, Ph. D., Instructor in History, Yale University, 233 Edwards St., New Haven, Conn.

ROBINSON, MISS FLORENCE PORTER, Head of Department of History, High School, 543 Marshall St., Milwaukee, Wis.

ROBINSON, GUSTAVUS HILL, A. B., 3632 Blaine Ave., St. Louis, Mo.

ROBINSON, JAMES HARVEY, Ph. D., Professor Columbia University, New York.

*ROBINSON, JANE BANCROFT (Mrs. Geo. O.), Ph. D., 425 Cass Ave., Detroit, Mich.

*ROBINSON, MORGAN POITIAUX, 113 South Third St., Richmond, Va.

ROCKWELL, WILLIAM WALKER, S. T. B., Lic. Theol., Assistant Professor of Church History, Union Theological Seminary, 700 Park Ave., New York, N. Y.

RODGERS, BRADLEY CARLETON, A. B., Principal of High School, Vergennes, Vt.

RODMAN, MISS MACY D., University of Chicago, Chicago, Ill.

ROGERS, HARRY, 2216 De Lancey St., Philadelphia, Pa.

ROGERS, REV. JAMES WILLIAM, A. M., Box 9, Walton, Boone Co., Ky.

ROLFE, PROF. HENRY WINCHESTER, Stanford University, Cal. (Pacific Coast Branch.)

ROLLER, HON. JOHN EDWIN, LL. B., LL. D., Harrisonburg, Va.

ROOSEVELT, HON. THEODORE, A. B., LL. D., President of the United States, Washington, D. C.

ROOT, GEORGE A., 133 Orange St., New Haven, Conn.

ROOT, ROBERT CROMWELL, B. S., A. M., 219 Grant Bldg., Los Angeles, Cal. (Pacific Coast Branch.)

ROOT, WINFRED T., 2209 Tioga St., Philadelphia, Pa.

ROSBOROUGH, C. R., Lock Box 174, Moline, Ill.

ROSE, ARTHUR P., Geneva, N. Y.

ROSE, JOHN CARTER, LL. B., Room 628 Equitable Bldg., Baltimore, Md.

ROSENDALE, HON. SIMON W., Vice-President American Jewish Historical Society, 57 State St., Albany, N. Y.

ROSENFELD, MAURICE, 1620 Michigan Ave., Chicago, Ill.

ROSENGARTEN, JOSEPH GEORGE, M. A., 1704 Walnut St., Philadelphia, Pa.

ROSS, DENMAN WALDO, Ph. D., Cambridge, Mass.

ROSS, WALTER LEE, A. M., Edmond, Okla.

ROWELL, MISS ELIZABETH, 1243 16th Ave., North, Seattle, Wash. (Pacific Coast Branch.)

ROWLAND, DUNBAR, B. S., LL. B., LL. D., Director Dept. of Archives and History, Jackson, Miss.

ROYAL HISTORICAL SOCIETY, 6 South Square, Gray's Inn, London, W. C., England.

ROYLAND, WILLIAM G., University of Utah, Salt Lake City, Utah.

ROYCE, JOSIAH, Ph. D., Professor Harvard University, Cambridge, Mass.

RUDD, CHANNING, D. C. L., Intercontinental Correspondence University, Washington, D. C.

RUDD, MALCOLM DAY, Lakeville, Conn.

RUGGLES, ALMA HAMMOND L'HOMMEDIEU, The Woodley, Columbia Road, Washington, D. C.

RULLKOETTER, WILLIAM, A. B., Ph. D., Professor Drury College, Springfield, Mo.

RUSSEL, GEORGE H., State Savings Bank, Detroit, Mich.

RUSSEL, HENRY, Michigan Central R. R. Co., Detroit, Mich.

RUSSELL, GEORGE SHELBY, care The Bank of Commerce, National Association, Cleveland, Ohio.

RUSSELL, HARRY U., 423 Wisconsin Ave., Madison, Wis.

RUSSELL, JAMES HERBERT, B. S., A. B., 940 Water St., Indiana, Pa.

RUSSELL, REV. WILLIAM T., 408 North Charles St., Baltimore, Md.

RUST, NATHANIEL JOHNSON, 488 Commonwealth Ave., Boston, Mass.

RUSTON, WILLIAM OTIS, D. D., Dubuque, Iowa.

RUTGERS COLLEGE LIBRARY, New Brunswick, N. J.

RUTLAND, JAMES RICHARD, A. B., Librarian Alabama Polytechnic Institute, Auburn, Ala.

RYAN, DANIEL J., Spahr Building, Columbus, Ohio.

RYAN, JOHN JOSEPH, A. M., Gilroy, Cal. (Pacific Coast Branch.)

SACHS, JULIUS, Ph. D., Teachers' College, Columbia University, New York, N. Y.

SACHSE, JULIUS FRIEDRICH, Litt. D., 4428 Pine St., Philadelphia, Pa.

*SALMON, LUCY MAYNARD, A. M., Poughkeepsie, N. Y.

SAMPSON, FRANCIS ASBURY, A. M., LL. B., Secretary State Historical Society of Missouri, Columbia, Mo.

SANBORN, JOHN BELL, M. L., Ph. D., Madison, Wis.

SANFORD, ALBERT HART, A. B., Stevens Point, Wis.

SAN FRANCISCO PUBLIC LIBRARY, San Francisco, Cal.

SANDERSON, EUGENE C., 407 East 12th St., Eugene, Ore. (Pacific Coast Branch.)

*SANGER, HON. WILLIAM CARY, A. M., LL. B., LL. D., Sangerfield, N. Y.

SARGENT, CARLA FERN, A. M., 627 Clark St., Evanston, Ill.

SARTELLE, EDWARD JAMES, 340 Main St., Worcester, Mass.

SAUNDERS, CHARLES GURLEY, A. M., 95 Milk St., Boston, Mass.

SAVIDGE, HON. WILLIAM, A. B., Spring Lake, Mich.

SAWYER, CHARLES B., 104 Jefferson Ave., Detroit, Mich.

SAYLER, JUNE ELLIOTT (Mrs. Harry L.), care Press Association of Chicago, 138 Jackson Boulevard, Chicago, Ill.

SCHAFER, JOSEPH, Ph. D., Head of History Department, University of Oregon, Eugene, Ore. (Pacific Coast Branch.)

SCHAFF, DAVID SCHLEY, D. D., The Western Theological Seminary, 737 Ridge Ave., Allegheny, Pa.

SCHELL, EDWIN ALLISON, Ph. D., Presiding Elder M. E. Church, 607 Wabash Ave., Crawfordsville, Ind.

SCHENCK, MRS. ELIZABETH HUBBELL, 2026 R St. N. W., Washington, D. C.

SCHERGER, GEORGE L., Ph. D., Professor of History, Armour Institute, Chicago, Ill.

SCHERR, HARRY, Williamson, W. Va.

SCHMIDT, ALFRED F. W., A. B., Librarian George Washington University, Washington, D. C.

SCHMIDT, F. G. G., 345 East 13th St., Eugene, Ore. (Pacific Coast Branch.)

SCHMIDT, PROFESSOR LOUIS BERNARD, Iowa State College, Ames, Iowa.

SCHMIDT, DR. OTTO L., 3328 Michigan Ave., Chicago, Ill.

SCHMITT, ALFRED C., A. M., Ph. D., Albany, Oregon.

SCHŒLKOPF, HENRY, 1700 Grand Ave., Milwaukee, Wis.

SCHOOLCRAFT, HENRY LAWRENCE, Ph. D., University of Illinois, Urbana, Ill.

*SCHOULER, JAMES, LL. D., 60 Congress St., Boston, Mass.

SCHUMACHER, BOWEN WISNER, A. B., 107 Dearborn St., Chicago, Ill.

SCHUYLER, LIVINGSTON ROWE, A. M., B. D., Ph. D., College of City of New York, New York, N. Y.

SCHUYLER, ROBERT L., 1025 Park Ave., New York, N. Y.

*SCHWILL, FERDINAND, Ph. D., Professor University of Chicago, Chicago, Ill.

*SCOTT, AUSTIN, LL. D., President Rutgers College, New Brunswick, N. J.

SCOTT, CLARENCE W., A. M., Professor New Hampshire College, Durham, N. H.

SCOTT, EBEN GREENOUGH, A. M., 324 S. Franklin St., Wilkes-Barre, Pa.

*SCOTT, HENRY EDWARDS, A. B., Medford High School, Medford, Mass.

SCOTT, HUGH MCDONALD, D. D., Professor Chicago Theological Seminary, 520 W. Adams St., Chicago, Ill.

SCRATCHLEY, REV. HENRY P., M. A., 60 Spruce St., Bloomfield, N. J.

SCRIBNER, WOODBURY J., Oak Park, Ill.

SCRIPTURE, ARTHUR M., A. M., C. E., Principal New Hartford High School, New Hartford, N. Y.

SEAGER, KARL'A., 171 W. 95th St., New York, N. Y.

SEARS, JOSEPH HAMBLIN, care Messrs. D. Appleton & Co., 436 5th Ave., New York, N. Y.

SEBRING, MISS EMMA G., St. Agatha's School, 557 West End Ave., New York, N. Y.

*SEDGWICK, LEE M., Rooms 7-8 Beals Bldg., Kansas City, Mo.

SEIDERS, C. A., 1915 Jefferson St., Toledo, Ohio..

SEIPP, MISS ALMA, 3300 Michigan Ave., Chicago, Ill.

SEIPP, WILLIAM C., Teutonic Bldg., 172 Washington St., Chicago, Ill.

SELBY, PAUL, 5468 Monroe Ave., Chicago, Ill.

SELIGMAN, EDWIN ROBERT ANDERSON, Ph. D., LL. D., Professor Columbia University, New York, N. Y.

SELLERY, GEO. CLARKE, Ph. D., Assistant Professor European History, University of Wisconsin, Madison, Wis.

SENNETT, LUCIEN FRANK, A. M., St. Albans, Knoxville, Ill.

SENNING, JOHN P., Central High School, Grand Forks, N. D.

SEVERANCE, ALLEN DUDLEY, A. M., Western Reserve University, Cleveland, Ohio.

SEVERANCE, FRANK HAYWARD, B. S., Secretary Buffalo Historical Society, 150 Jewett Ave., Buffalo, N. Y.

SEWALL, JOTHAM BRADBURY, A. M., D. D., 1501 Beacon St., Brookline, Mass.

SEWARD, GEN. WILLIAM HENRY, Auburn, N. Y.

SEYMOUR, HON. HORATIO, A. M., Utica, N. Y.

SEYMOUR, MORRIS WOODRUFF, LL. B., Bridgeport, Conn.

SHAHAN, THOMAS JOSEPH, D. D., Professor Catholic University of America, Washington, D. C.

SHAMBAUGH, BENJAMIN FRANKLIN, Ph. D., Professor State University, Iowa City, Iowa.

SHANNON, HON. RICHARD CUTTS, LL.D., Brockport, N. Y.

SHARP, GEORGE M., Judge Supreme Bench of Baltimore, 2105 St. Paul St., Baltimore, Md.

SHAW, ALBERT, Ph. D., LL. D., Editor *The American Monthly Review of Reviews*, 13 Astor Place, New York.

SHAW, MISS EMMA G., care Miss A. F. Foster, Centre Sandwich, N. H.

SHAW, OLIVER W., President First National Bank, Austin, Minn.

SHEARER, AUGUSTUS HUNT, Ph. D., Dartmouth College, Hanover, N. H.

SHEARER, JOHNS LOUIS, A. M., President of Faculty, The Ohio Mechanics Institute, Cincinnati, Ohio.

SHELDON, HENRY DAVIDSON, Eugene, Ore. (Pacific Coast Branch.)

SHEPARDSON, FRANCIS WAYLAND, Ph. D., LL. D., 5592 Kimbark Ave., Chicago, Ill.

SHEPHERD, WILLIIAM ROBERT, Ph. D., Columbia University, New York.

SHERMAN, GORDON E., Ph. B., Morristown, N. J.

SHERMAN, ROGER, Room 901, 135 Adams St., Chicago, Ill.

SHERRICK, MISS SARAH MARGARET, Ph. D., Lock Box 10, Westerville, Ohio.

SHERRILL, M. O., State Librarian, Raleigh, N. C.

SHERWOOD, MISS ELIZABETH LEE, B. A., 254 Prospect St., New Haven, Conn.

SHINN, CHARLES HOWARD, A. B., Forest Supervisor North Sierra Reserve, North Fork, Cal. (Pacific Coast Branch.)

SHIPLEY, MISS HANNAH T., The Misses Shipley's School, Bryn Mawr, Pa.'

SHIPMAN, ARTHUR L., A. B., LL. B., 750 Main St., Hartford, Conn.

SHIPMAN, HENRY ROBINSON, Ph. D., Princeton, N. J.

SHIPPEN, MRS. REBECCA LLOYD, 209 Monument St., West, Baltimore, Md.

SHIRAS, HON. GEORGE, 3d, LL. B., Pittsburgh, Pa.

SHIRAS, HON. GEORGE, Jr., LL. D., Associate Justice U. S. Supreme Court, Washington, D. C.

SHIVELEY, CHARLES ARTHUR, State Normal School, Hayes, Kansas.

SHORT, EDWARD MARIAN, Bloomington, Neb.

SHORTT, ADAM, A. M., Professor Queens University, Kingston, Ontario, Canada.

SHOTWELL, JAMES THOMSON, Ph. D., *The Times*, London, Eng.

SHOW, ARLEY BARTHLOW, A. M., B. D., Professor Stanford University, Cal. (Pacific Coast Branch.)

SIEBERT, WILBUR HENRY, A. M., Professor of European History, Ohio State University, Columbus, Ohio.

SILL, PROF. HENRY A., A. M., Ph. D., Cornell University, Ithaca, N. Y.

SILVER, JOHN ARCHER, Ph. D., Professor in Hobart College, Geneva, N. Y.

SIMMONS COLLEGE LIBRARY, Boston, Mass.

SIMONS, SARAH E., care Board of Education, Washington, D. C.

SIMPSON, SAMUEL, Ph. D., 250 Collins St., Hartford, Conn.

SINGER, EDWARD T., 403 East Superior St., Chicago, Ill.

SINNICKSON, LOUISE E. B. (Mrs. Andrew), Salem, N. J.

SINSABAUGH, MISS ETTA, A. M., 289 State St., Springfield, Mass.

SIOUSSAT, MRS. ANNIE MIDDLETON LEAKEN, Vice-President Arundell Club, Lake Roland, Baltimore Co., Md.

Sioussat, St. George L., Ph. D., Professor of History and Economics, University of the South, Sewanee, Tenn.

Slade, Louis Palmer, A. M., Chicopee High School, Chicopee, Mass.

Slater, Bertha E., 765 Oak St., Eugene, Ore. (Pacific Coast Branch.)

*Slattery, John Richard, 12 rue Cernuschi, Paris, France.

*Sloane, William Milligan, Ph. D., L. H. D., LL. D., Professor Columbia University; Secretary Academy of Political Science, New York.

Slocum, Charles E., M. D., Defiance, O.

Slocum, Hon. Elliott Truax, A. B., A. M., Detroit, Mich.

Smetanka, Jaroslav, 41 E. 69th St., New York, N. Y.

Smiley, Hon. Charles Henry, New Bloomfield, Pa.

Smith, Alexander Latta, A. B., 51 Produce Exchange, Toledo, Ohio.

Smith, Charles Card, A. M., Treasurer Massachusetts Historical Society, 286 Marlborough St., Boston, Mass.

Smith, Charles Henry, LL. D., Professor Yale University, New Haven, Conn.

Smith, Charles Wesley, A. B., B. L. S., University of Washington Library, Seattle, Wash.

Smith College Library, Northampton, Mass.

Smith, Don E., A. B., Faculty Club, Berkeley, Cal. (Pacific Coast Branch.)

Smith, Edward B., Nickerson College, Nickerson, Kan.

Smith, Edward James, care Spaulding & Co., Chicago, Ill.

Smith, Miss Elvira Bush, Brighton High School, Boston, Mass.

Smith, Ernest Ashton, Ph. D., Professor Allegheny College, Meadville, Pa.

Smith, Mrs. Frederick A., 87 Rush St., Chicago, Ill.

*Smith, Goldwin, D. C. L., LL. D., Toronto, Ontario, Canada.

Smith, James Cosslett, A. M., Detroit, Mich.

Smith, John M. C., Charlotte, Mich.

Smith, John Weitzel Forney, D. C. L., 816 4th St. N. W., Washington, D. C.

Smith, Justin Harvey, A. M., Professor Dartmouth College, Hanover, N. H.

Smith, Miss Mary Shannon, A. B., Elmcroft Lee, Mass.

Smith, Milton W., 413 Failing Building, Portland, Ore. (Pacific Coast Branch.)

Smith, Preserved, 419 West 118th St., New York, N. Y.

Smith, Theodore Clarke, Ph. D., Williamstown, Mass.

Smith, Hon. Thomas Guilford, A. M., C. E., LL. D., Buffalo, N. Y.

Smith, Walter M., Librarian University of Wisconsin, Madison, Wis.

Smith, Walter R., Washington University, St. Louis, Mo.

Smith, Hon. William Alden, Grand Rapids, Mich.

Smith, W. Roy, Ph. D., Bryn Mawr College, Bryn Mawr, Pa.

Snavely, Charles, Ph. D., Otterbein University, Westerville, Ohio.

Snow, Marshall Solomon, A. M., Professor of History, Washington University, St. Louis, Mo.

Snowden, Clinton A., M. A., Tacoma, Wash.

Snowden, Yeates, Charleston, S. C.

Snyder, Major Henry Daniel, U. S. A., Essex Junction, Vt.

Social Law Library, Court House, Boston, Mass.

Soley, James Russell, LL. B., 35 Wall St., New York, N. Y.

Sollers, Basil, Principal Baltimore Training School for Teachers, 1530 Harlem Ave., Baltimore, Md.

Solomon, Mrs. Hannah G., 4406 Michigan Ave., Chicago, Ill.

Sommers, Henry Stern, B. L., 189 E. Fourth St., St. Paul, Minn.

Sommerville, Rev. Charles William, A. B., Sc. B., A. M., Ph. D., 1413 Hollins St., Baltimore, Md.

Soper, Alexander Coburn, A. M., Lakewood, N. J.

Sowdon, Arthur John Clark, A. B., LL. B., A. M., Governor Massachusetts Society Colonial Wars, 66 Beacon St., Boston, Mass.

Spaeth, Adolph, D. D., LL. D., Mt. Airy, Pa.

Sparks, Edwin Erle, Ph. D., Professor University of Chicago, Chicago, Ill.

Sparrow, Miss Caroline L., A. B., 11 South Laurel St., Richmond, Va.

Speer, Emory, LL. D., Judge U. S. District Court, Southern District of Georgia, Macon, Ga.

Spencer, Charles Worthen, Princeton, N. J.

Spencer, Henry Russell, A. M., 24 Mercer St., Princeton, N. J.

Spencer, John Oakley, Ph. D., President Morgan College, Baltimore, Md.

Spiegelberg, F., 15 William St., New York, N. Y.

Spofford, Ainsworth Rand, LL. D., Vice-President Columbia Historical Society; Library of Congress, Washington, D. C.

Sprague, George Clare, 191 Berkley Place, Brooklyn, N. Y.

*Sprague, Rufus F., Greenville, Montcalm Co., Mich.

Spring, Leverett Wilson, D. D., Professor Williams College, Williamstown, Mass.

Stagg, Miss Pauline H., 384 Valley Road, West Orange, N. J.

Stanard, William G., Corresponding Secretary and Librarian Virginia Historical Society, 13 Beech St., Richmond, Va.

Stanclift, Henry Clay, Ph. D., Professor Cornell College, Mount Vernon, Iowa.

Stanley, Kate, 32 Linden St., Brookline, Mass.

STANWOOD, EDWARD, Editorial Rooms, *Youth's Companion*, Boston, Mass.

STARR, MISS MARY ISABELLA, A. B., Oaksmere, Davenport's Neck, New Rochelle, N. Y.

START, MISS CORA ANGELINE, A. M., 58 Früit St., Worcester, Mass.

START, EDWIN AUGUSTUS, A. M., Billerica, Mass.

STATE LIBRARY, Lansing, Mich.

STATE NORMAL SCHOOL, San Diego, Cal.

STATE NORMAL SCHOOL, Stevens Point, Wis.

ST. CHARLES COLLEGE LIBRARY, Ellicott City, Md.

STEARNS, WALLACE NELSON, A. M., B. D., Ph. D., Professor of Languages, Wesley College, Grand Forks, N. D.

STEELE, JAMES DALLAS, B. D., Ph. D., 15 Grove Terrace, Passaic, N. J.

STEINER, BERNARD CHRISTIAN, Ph. D., LL. B., Librarian Enoch Pratt Free Library; Associate, Johns Hopkins University; formerly Dean Baltimore Law School, Baltimore, Md.

STEPHENS, FRANK FLETCHER, 633 S. 49th St., Philadelphia, Pa.

*STEPHENS, HENRY MORSE, A. M., Professor University of California, Berkeley, Cal. (Pacific Coast Branch.)

STEPHENS, W. HUDSON, Lowville, N. Y.

STEPHENSON, HON. SAMUEL M., Menominee, Mich.

STETSON, FRANCIS LYNDE, LL. B., A. M., 4 E. 74th St., New York.

STEVENS, HARRY EUGENE, 26 E. Cedar Ave., Merchantville, N. J.

STEVENS, MISS MAUD FRANCES, A. M., Palo Alto, Cal. (Pacific Coast Branch.)

STEVENS, PLOWDON, JR., B. S., 2126 Washington Ave., New York, N. Y.

STEVENSON, EDWARD LUTHER, Ph. D., Professor Rutgers College, New Brunswick, N. J.

STEVENSON, ROBERT TAYLOR, Department of History, Ohio Wesleyan University, Delaware, Ohio.

STEWARD, MISS MABEL ALICE, A. M., 560 Cass Ave., Detroit, Mich.

STEWART, CHARLES W., Superientendent Library and Naval War Records, Navy Department, Washington, D. C.

STEWART, HON. JOHN, Chambersburg, Pa.

STEWART, HON. LISPENARD, A. B., LL. B., 6 Fifth Ave., New York.

STICKLES, ARNDT M., A. M., 314 Chandler Ave., Evansville, Ind.

STIMPSON, HERBERT B., 207 North Calvert St., Baltimore, Md.

STIMSON, HON. RODNEY METCALF, A. M., Treasurer Marietta College, Marietta, Ohio.

STOCKBRIDGE, HON. HENRY, LL. B., 11 N. Calhoun St., Baltimore, Md.

STODDARD, MRS. JULIA SUMNER CREWITT, A. M., Belfast, Me.

*STOECKEL, CARL, A. M., Norfolk, Conn.

STOKES, REV. ANSON PHELPS, Jr., A. M., Yale University, New Haven, Conn.

*STOKES, WILLIAM E. D., 73d St. and Broadway, New York.

STONE, ALFRED HOLT, 200 A St. S. E., Washington, D. C.

STONE, CHARLES WARREN, A. B., President Warren County Historical Society, Warren, Pa.

STONE, EDWIN PEARSON, Saginaw, Mich.

STONE, HON. JOHN WESLEY, Marquette, Mich.

STONE, LINCOLN RIPLEY, M. D., 131 Vernon St., Newton, Mass.

STONE, MISS MARY A., Teacher of History, High School, Cambridge, Ohio.

STORMS, REV. ALFRED BOYNTON, A. M., D. D., LL. D., President Iowa State College, Ames, Iowa.

STORY, LESSEPS, 303 Baronne St., New Orleans, La.

STOWE, REV. WILBUR FISKE, D. D., 32 Church St., Saugerties, N. Y.

STOWELL, ROY SHERMAN, A. M., 132 Warwick Ave., Rochester, N. Y.

STRASSBURG UNIVERSITATS UND LANDESBIBLIOTHEK, Strassburg, Germany.

STRATTON, MISS HENRIETTA GIBBON, Western College for Women, Oxford, Ohio.

STRAUB, JOHN, Eugene, Ore. (Pacific Coast Branch.)

STRAUS, HON. OSCAR SOLOMON, L. H. D., LL. D., Secretary of Commerce and Labor, 2600 16th St., N. W., Washington, D. C.

STRAUS, PERCY SELDEN, A. B., 46 W. 71st St., New York, N. Y.

STREET, OLIVER DAY, A. B., LL. B., Guntersville, Ala.

STREETER, FRANK SHERWIN, A. B., 77 N. Main St., Concord, N. H.

STRONG, FRANK, Ph. D., Chancellor University of Kansas, Lawrence, Kan.

STROOCK, SOL. M., A. M., LL. B., 320 Broadway, New York, N. Y.

STRYKER, MISS FLORENCE ELIZABETH, A. B., Nntional Park Seminary, Forest Glen, Md.

STUBBERT, MISS MARY REED WYMAN, 140 Broad St., Bloomfield, N. J.

STURGIS, CHARLES F., 209 Adams St., Chicago, Ill.

*SULLIVAN, FRANK J., S. E. Van Ness Ave. and Washington St., San Francisco, Cal. (Pacific Coast Branch.)

SULLIVAN, JAMES, Ph. D., 308 W. 97th St., New York.

SUMNER, GEORGE FREDERICK, Canton Junction, Mass.

SUMNER, GEORGE STEDMAN, Ph. D., Claremont, Cal. (Pacific Coast Branch.)

SUMNER, JOHN OSBORNE, 225 Marlborough St., Boston, Mass.

SUPER, CHARLES WILLIAM, LL. D., Ohio University, Athens, Ohio.

SUTHERLAND, GEORGE GEER, A. B., 256 Park Place, Janesville, Wis.

SUTLIFF, MISS PHEBE TEMPERANCE, A. M., 234 High St., Warren, Ohio.

SWAIN, HENRY H., Ph. D., President of Montana State Normal College, Dillon, Mont.

SWAN, ROBERT THAXTER, Commissioner of Public Records, State House, Boston, Mass.

SWANGER, FRANCIS ASBURY, M. S. D., A. M., Superintendent of Public Schools, Anaconda, Mont.

SWEENEY, J. D., Red Bluff, Cal. (Pacific Coast Branch.)

SWIFT, CHARLES M., 80 Griswold St., Detroit, Mich.

SWIFT, LINDSAY, 388 Park St., West Roxbury, Mass.

SWISHER, PROFESSOR CHARLES S., George Washington University, Washington, D. C.

SYMMES, FRANK JAMESON, 630 Harrison St., San Francisco, Cal. (Pacific Coast Branch.)

SYRACUSE UNIVERSITY HISTORICAL ASSOCIATION, Hall of Languages, Syracuse, N. Y.

SZE, SAO-KE ALFRED, A. B., M. A., Chinese Merchant Steam Navigation Co., Hankow, China.

TAFT, HON. ROYAL CHAPIN, A. M., Providence, R. I.

*TALBOT, MISS MARION, A. M., LL. D., Professor and Dean University of Chicago, Chicago, Ill.

TALBOTT, MRS. LAURA OSBORNE, The Lennox, 1523 L St., Washington, D. C.

TALCOTT, MISS MARY KINGSBURY, Registrar Connecticut Society of Colonial Dames, 133 Sigourney St., Hartford, Conn.

TALKINGTON, HENRY LEONIDAS, A. M., Professor of Civics and History, State Normal School, Lewiston, Idaho.

TARBELL, MISS IDA MINERVA, A. M., 141 E. 25th St., New York.

TAUSSIG, RUDOLPH J., 28 Main St., San Francisco, Cal. (Pacific Coast Branch.)

TAYLOR, CALVIN HILL, A. B., Union, Neb.

TAYLOR, CHARLES SUMNER, A. B., 430 Waveland Ave., Chicago, Ill.

TAYLOR, EDWARD F., 448 Prospect Place, Brooklyn, N. Y.

TAYLOR, MISS JANE (present address uncertain).

TAYLOR, JOHN METCALF, A. M., 36 Pearl St., Hartford, Conn.

TAYLOR, WILLIAM IRVEN, A. M., Gosport, Ind.

TEGGART, FREDERICK JOHN, A. B., 31 Post St., San Francisco, Cal. (Pacific Coast Branch.)

TEMPE NORMAL SCHOOL LIBRARY, Tempe, Ariz.

TEMPLE, HENRY WILLIAM, D. D., Washington and Jefferson College, Washington, Pa.

TEMPLE, W. F., M. D., 240 Huntington Ave., Boston, Mass.

*TENNEY, HENRY ALLEN, LL. B., P. O. Box F, Patchogue, N. Y.

TERRY, BENJAMIN STITES, Ph. D., LL. D., Professor University of Chicago, Chicago, Ill.

TERRY, JAMES, 78 Weathersfield Ave., Hartford, Conn.

TEXTOR, LUCY ELIZABETH, Ph. D., Vassar College, Poughkeepsie, N. Y.

*THALHEIMER, MISS MARY ELSIE, Avondale, Cincinnati, Ohio.

THATCHER, OLIVER J., Ph. D., Professor University of Chicago, Chicago, Ill.

THAXTER, MAJOR SIDNEY W., A. B., Portland, Me.

THAYER, SAMUEL R., LL. D., 707 East Main St., Rochester, N. Y.

THAYER, WILLIAM ROSCOE, A. M., 8 Berkeley St., Cambridge, Mass.

THOMAS, ALLEN CLAPP, A. M., Professor of History and Librarian Haverford College, Haverford, Pa.

THOMAS, DAVID YANCEY, Ph. D., 304 East Orange St., Gainesville, Fla.

THOMAS, ISAAC, A. B., A. M., Principal of High School, Burlington, Vt.

*THOMPSON, MISS ANNA BOYNTON, A. B., A. M., Litt. D., Thayer Academy, South Braintree, Mass.

THOMPSON, CARTER SEVIER, 429 Arch St., Philadelphia, Pa.

THOMPSON, MISS CLARA MILDRED, A. B., Whittier Hall, 1230 Amsterdam Ave., New York, N.Y. (June 1 to Oct. 1, 44 E. Cain St., Atlanta, Ga.)

THOMPSON, FRANCIS McGEE, Judge of Probate Court of Franklin County, Greenfield, Mass.

THOMPSON, FREDERIC LINCOLN, care Dr. W. S. Thompson, Augusta, Me.

THOMPSON, GEORGE C., Ph. D., 2159 Clinton Ave., Alameda, Cal. (Pacific Coast Branch.)

THOMPSON, JAMES WESTFALL, Ph. D., Professor University of Chicago, Chicago, Ill.

THOMPSON, MISS LAURA A., Library of Congress, Washington, D. C.

THOMPSON, MRS. LIDA BALDWIN, 2159 Clinton Ave., Alameda, Cal. (Pacific Coast Branch.)

THOMPSON, ROBERT ELLIS, S. T. D., Central High School, Philadelphia, Pa.

THOMPSON, THOMAS C., 56 Times Bldg., Chattanooga, Tenn.

THOMPSON, T. P., 1812 Calhoun St., New Orleans, La.

THOMSON, MISS FRANCES E., High School, Medina, O.

THOMSON, JOHN, Librarian Free Library, 1217 Chestnut St., Philadelphia, Pa.

THORNDIKE, EVERETT LYNN, A. B., A. M., School of Political Science, Columbia University, New York, N. Y.

THORPE, FRANCIS NEWTON, Ph. D., Mt. Holly, N. J.

THORSTENBERG, HERMAN J., University of Oklahoma, Norman, Okla.

THURBER, CHARLES HERBERT, Ph. D., care Ginn & Co., 29 Beacon St., Boston, Mass.

THWAITES, REUBEN GOLD, LL. D., Secretary and Superintendent State Historical Society of Wisconsin, Madison, Wis.

THWING, CHARLES F., D. D., LL. D., President Western Reserve University and Adelbert College, Cleveland, Ohio.

TIDBALL, REV. THOS. ALLEN, D. D., University of the South, Sewanee, Tenn.

TIFFANY, ARCHDEACON CHARLES COMFORT, D. D., 29 Lafayette Place, New York, N. Y.

TIFFANY, ORRIN EDWARD, A. B., A. M., Ph. D., Professor of History and Economics, Western Maryland College, Westminster, Md.

TIGHE, AMBROSE, German American Bank Bldg., St. Paul, Minn.

TILLINGHAST, CALEB BENJAMIN, A. M., Librarian State Library, State House, Boston, Mass.

TILLINGHAST, WILLIAM HOPKINS, A. B., Assistant Librarian Harvard University, Cambridge, Mass.

TILTON, ASA CURRIER, Ph. D., University of Wisconsin, 21 Mendota Court, Madison, Wis.

TODD, GEORGE DAVIDSON, 31 St. James Court, Louisville, Ky.

TODD, JOHN R., Hartley Hall, 115th St. and Amsterdam Ave., New York, N. Y.

TOLL, JANE BEAN (Mrs. A. C.), A. B., 1374 12th Ave., Sunset District, San Francisco, Cal.

TOMPKINS, EUGENE, 325 Commonwealth Ave., Boston, Mass.

TOMPKINS, HAMILTON BULLOCK, A. M., LL. B., Vice-President Newport, R. I., Historical Society, 229 Broadway, New York.

TORRANCE, WILLIAM CLAYTON, 104 North 5th St., Richmond, Va.

TOWAR, EDGAR H., Box 30, Station N, New York, N. Y.

TOWNSEND, HOWARD, A. B., 32 Nassau St., New York.

TOWNSEND, JOHN W., 594 Howard Ave., New Haven, Conn.

TRASK, T. C., B. A., M. A., High School of Commerce, 155 W. 65th St., New York, N. Y.

TRAVIS, IRA DUDLEY, Ph. D., 1116 Second St., Salt Lake City, Utah.

*TRAYLOR, ROBERT LEE, Box 324, Memphis, Tenn.

TREAT, JOHN HARVEY, Lawrence, Mass.

TREAT, PAYSON JACKSON, A. M., Stanford University, Cal. (Pacific Coast Branch.)

*TREE, HON. LAMBERT, 70 La Salle St., Chicago, Ill.

TRE FETHREN, EUGENE BYRON, A. B., B. D., Waubay, S. Dak.

TREMAIN, MISS MARY, 1318 R St., Lincoln, Neb.

TRENHOLME, NORMAN MACLAREN, A. M., Ph. D., University of Missouri, 707 Maryland Place, Columbia, Mo.

TRENT, WILLIAM PETERFIELD, A. M., Professor Columbia University, New York.

TRIMBLE, MISS CLARA E., A. B., Urbana High School, Urbana, Ill.

TRIMBLE, WILLIAM JOSEPH, 3524 West Second St., Spokane, Wash. (Pacific Coast Branch.)

TRINITY COLLEGE LIBRARY, Durham, N. C.

TROEGER, JOHN W., 112 N. Spring Ave., La Grange, Ill.

TROUP, HON. JAMES O., Bowling Green, Ohio.

TROUT, CATHERINE J., 1025 Warren Ave., Chicago, Ill.

TROWBRIDGE, FRANCIS BACON, LL. B., 353 Temple St., New Haven, Conn.

TRUMBULL, JONATHAN, The Otis Library, Norwich, Conn.

TUCKER, MISS ALICE BLYTHE, A. M., Adelphi College, Brooklyn, N. Y.

*TUCKER, GEORGE FOX, Ph. D., 615 and 616 Barristers' Hall, Boston, Mass.

TUCKER, HENRY R., A. B., A. M., Instructor in History, William McKinley High School, 3529 California Ave., St. Louis, Mo.

TUCKERMAN, BAYARD, A. B., 59 Wall St., New York.

TUCKERMAN, FREDERICK, Ph., D., Amherst, Mass.

TUELL, MISS HARRIET EMILY, Ph. D., 10 Harvard Place, Somerville, Mass.

TUFTS COLLEGE LIBRARY, Tufts College, Mass.

TURNER, CHARLES W., Associate Professor of Law, University of Tennessee, Knoxville, Tenn.

TURNER, FREDERICK JACKSON, Ph. D., Professor University of Wisconsin, Madison, Wis.

TURNER, WALLACE MANAAN, 12 Glenwood Ave., Newton Centre, Mass.

TUTHILL, JAMES EDWARD, A. M., University of Minnesota, Minneapolis, Minn.

TYLER, LYON GARDINER, LL. D., President William and Mary College, Williamsburg, Va.

TYLER, MASON WHITING, A. B., Marrietta College, Marietta, Ohio.

ULMANN, ALBERT, B. S., Trustee Amer. Scenic and Hist. Pres. Soc., 40 Exchange Place, New York.

UMBACH, S. L., D. D., Professor of History and Practical Theology, Union Biblical Institute, Naperville, Ill.

UNIVERSITY OF CINCINNATI LIBRARY, Cincinnati, Ohio.

UNIVERSITY OF MAINE LIBRARY, Orono, Me.

UNIVERSITY OF MISSOURI LIBRARY, Columbia, Mo.

UNIVERSITY OF NEBRASKA LIBRARY, Lincoln, Neb.

UNIVERSITY OF THE PACIFIC LIBRARY, San Jose, Cal. (Pacific Coast Branch.)

UPHAM, WARREN, A. M., D. Sc., Secretary Minnesota Historical Society, St. Paul, Minn.

USHER, ELLIS B., Wells Building, Milwaukee, Wis.

*U. S. NAVAL WAR COLLEGE, Newport, R. I.

UTLEY, EDWARD HUNTINGTON, care Bessemer and Lake Erie R. R. Co., Pittsburgh, Pa.

UTLEY, JESEPH SIMEON, Conway, Ark.

VAIL, HENRY HOBART, LL. D., 322 W. 75th St., New York.

VALENTINE, EDWARD P., Richmond, Va.

VAN CLEEF, HENRY H., 58 Market St., Poughkeepsie, N. Y.

VAN DEVENTER, CYRUS CLARKE, A. M., Kingman, Kan.

VAN DYKE, PAUL, D. D., Professor Princeton University, Princeton, N. J.

VAN EVERA, JOHN R., Marquette, Mich.

VAN LOON, HENDRICK WILLIAM, Nouo Jasna, 2b, Warsaw, Russia.

VAN SICKLE, JAMES H., A. M., 1519 Linden Ave., Baltimore, Md.

VAN TYNE, CLAUDE HALSTEAD, Ph. D., 1105 E. University Ave., Ann Arbor, Mich.

VAN VLISSINGEN, PETER, Calumet Club, Chicago, Ill.

VASSAR COLLEGE LIBRARY, Poughkeepsie, N. Y.

VAUGHAN, WILLIAM JAMES, LL. D., Librarian Vanderbilt University, Nashville, Tenn.

VELASQUEZ DE LA CADENA, MISS MARIANA, 28 S. Maple Ave., East Orange, N. J.

VIGNAUD, HENRY, Secretary to the American Embassy, 18 Avenue Kleber, Paris, France.

VILES, JONAS, Ph. D., Instructor in History, University of Missouri, Columbia, Mo.

VILLARD, OSWALD GARRISON, A. M., P. O. Box 794, New York, N. Y.

VINCENT, HON. GEORGE ANDREW, 314 Main St., Fairmont, West Va.

VINCENT, GEORGE EDGAR, Ph. D., Professor University of Chicago, 5737 Lexington Ave., Chicago, Ill.

VINCENT, JOHN MARTIN, Ph. D., LL. D., Professor Johns Hopkins University, Baltimore, Md.

VIOLETTE, EUGENE MORROW, A. B., A. M., 5 Howland St., Cambridge Mass.

VIRGINIA STATE LIBRARY, Richmond, Va.

VIRTUE, GEORGE OLIEN, Ph. D., 754 W. Broadway, Winona, Minn.

VONDERSAAR, LULU CAROLINE, A. B., Teacher of History, High School 1205 Fourth Ave., North, Great Falls, Mont.

VROMAN, CHARLES EDWARD, Ph. D., LL. B., First National Bank Bldg., Chicago, Ill.

WACKER, CHARLES H., 410 Western Union Bldg., Chicago, Ill.

WADE, JEPTHA HOMER, Wade Bldg., Cleveland, Ohio.

WADSWORTH, MISS ALICE E., B. L., 6414 Lexington Ave., Chicago, Ill.

WAGNER, JOHN URBAN, Ph. B., 321 Taylor Ave., Scranton, Pa.

WAGONER, MRS. LUTHER, 849 Chestnut St., San Francisco, Cal. (Pacific Coast Branch.)

WAKEMAN, GEORGE BULKELEY, Ph. D., Moodus, Conn.

WALDO, DWIGHT BRYANT, A. M., Western State Normal School, Kalamazoo, Mich.

WALKER, ALBERT PERRY, A. M., Normal High School, Boston, Mass.

WALKER, BRYANT, A. B., Detroit, Mich.

WALKER, CURTIS HOWE, B. A., Ph. D., Instructor Yale University, New Haven, Conn.

WALKER, WILLISTON, Ph. D., D. D., Professor Yale University, New Haven, Conn.

WALLACE, DAVID DUNCAN, A. M., Ph. D., Wofford College, Spartanburg, S. C.

WALMSLEY, JAMES ELLIOTT, A. M., Ph. D., Millsaps College, Jackson, Miss.

WALRATH, MARTIN H., A. M., Principal High School, Box 544, Troy, N. Y.

WALSWORTH, ROSCOE, 35 Orchard St., Beachmont, Mass.

WALTER, JOSHUA J., Eugene, Ore. (Pacific Coast Branch.)

WALTON, JOSEPH S., Ph. D., Principal George School, George School, Pa.

*WALWORTH, MRS. ELLEN HARDIN, Saratoga, N. Y.

WARD, BROWNLEE ROBERTSON, 231 York St., New Haven, Conn.

WARD, GEORGE WASHINGTON, Ph. D., Principal Maryland State Normal School, Baltimore. Md.

WARFIELD, ETHELBERT DUDLEY, LL. D., President Lafayette College, Easton, Pa.

WARREN, H. LANGFORD, A. M., Professor of Architecture, Harvard University, 64 Oxford St., Cambridge, Mass.

WARREN, DR. JOHN COLLINS, A. B., M. D., LL. D., Hon. F. R. C. S., 58 Beacon St., Boston, Mass.

WARREN, JOSEPH PARKER, Ph. D., 27 North Hall, University of Chicago Chicago, Ill.

WASHINGTON COUNTY HISTORICAL SOCIETY, Washington, Pa.

WATERMAN, ARBA N., 40 Groveland Park, Chicago, Ill.

WATERS, WILLARD O., Library of Congress, 2514 13th St. N. W.; Washington, D. C.

WATROUS, GEORGE DUTTON, D. C., L., 121 Church St., New Haven, Conn.

WATSON, HON. DAVID K., A. B., LL. B., Member of the Commission to revise the laws of the United States, Bond Bldg., Washington, D. C.

WATSON, COL. JAMES TOMPKINS, Clinton, N. Y.

*WATSON, PAUL BARRON, A. B., Milton, Mass.

WATTLES, J. S., Civil Engineer, Missouri Valley, Iowa.

WATTS, MISS JENNY CHAMBERLAIN, M. A., 6 Exeter Park, Cambridge, Mass. .

WAUGH, JAMES CHURCH, 5012 Twelfth Ave., N. E., University Station, Washington.

WAY, ROYAL BRUNSON, Ph. D., Teacher of History, Northwestern University, 1633 Oak Ave., Evanston, Ill.

WAYNE COUNTY INDIANA HISTORICAL SOCIETY, Richmond, Ind.

WEATHERLY, ULYSSES GRANT, Ph. D., Professor Indiana State University, Bloomington, Ind.

WEAVER, EMILY P., 26 Bernard Ave., Toronto, Ontario, Canada.

WEBER, MRS. JESSIE PALMER, Librarian Illinois State Historical Library, Springfield, Ill.

WEBER, JOHN LANGDON, D. D., Litt. D., President Kentucky Wesleyan College, Winchester, Ky.

WEBSTER, HOMER J., Mount Union College, Alliance, Ohio.

WEED, RT. REV. EDWIN G., D. D., Jacksonville, Fla.

*WEEDEN, WILLIAM BABCOCK, A. M., 158 Waterman St., Providence, R. I.

WEEKS, STEPHEN BEAUREGARD, Ph. D., LL D., Superintendent U. S. Indian Industrial School, San Carlos, Arizona.

WEIK, JESSE W., Greencastle, Ind.

WEIMER, WALTER EARLE, 724 Cumberland St., Lebanon, Pa.

WEINSTEIN, HARRY I., 909 Western Ave., Seattle, Wash.

WEINSTOCK, HARRIS, 400 K St., Sacramento, Cal. (Pacific Coast Branch.)

WEISE, ARTHUR JAMES, A. M., 846 President St., Brooklyn, N. Y.

WELCH, MISS JANE MEADE, The Algonquin, Johnson Park, Buffalo, N. Y.

WELCH, MISS MARY D., Principal of High School, Mishawaka, Ind.

WELD, STEPHEN MINOT, A. M., Wareham, Mass.

WELLINGTON, RAYNOR G., A. M., 320 Walnut Ave., Boston, Mass.

WELLS COLLEGE LIBRARY, Aurora, N. Y.

WELLS, FREDERICK LATIMER, 116 S. Clinton St., Chicago, Ill.

WELLS, LOUIS R., A. M., 65 Hammond St., Cambridge, Mass.

WELLS, PHILIP PATTERSON, Ph. D., Forest Service, Washington, D. C.

WELTON, FRANK, National City Bank, Grand Rapids, Mich.

WENDELL, BARRETT, Professor Harvard University, 358 Marlborough St., Boston, Mass.

WERGELAND, MISS AGNES MATHILDE, Ph. D., Laramie, Wyo. (Pacific Coast Branch.)

WESLEYAN UNIVERSITY LIBRARY, Middletown, Conn.

WEST VIRGINIA UNIVERSITY LIBRARY, Morgantown, W. Va.

WEST, WILLIS MASON, A. M., Professor University of Minnesota, Minneapolis, Minn.

WESTERMANN, DR. WILLIAM LINN, 8 Florence Court, S. E., Minneapolis, Minn.

WESTERN STATE NORMAL SCHOOL, Kalamazoo, Mich.

WESTWOOD, REV. WILLIAM, Vice-President College of Emporia, 1213 Rural St., Emporia, Kan.

*WETMORE, HON. GEORGE PEABODY, A. B., A. M., LL. D., Newport, R. I.

WEYAND, REV. PAUL, A. B., 303 Miller St., Pittsburg, Pa.

WHEELER, ARTHUR MARTIN, A. M., LL. D., Professor Yale University, New Haven, Conn.

WHEELER, HORACE L., M. A., B. D., Boston Public Library, Boston, Mass.

WHEELER, ORVILLE S., care G. P. Putnams Sons, 27 W. 23d St., New York, N. Y.

WHEELER, SAMUEL H., Fairfield, Conn.

WHEELOCK, ARTHUR NEWHALL, A. M., City Superintendent of Schools, Riverside, Cal. (Pacific Coast Branch.)

WHEELWRIGHT, WILLIAM D., Portland, Ore. (Pacific Coast Branch.)

WHINERY, CHARLES CRAWFORD, A. M., 45 Glenwood Ave., East Orange, N. J.

WHIPPLE, ENOCH ALBERT, Grand Pacific Hotel, Chicago, Ill.

WHIPPLE, MISS MARY ELLA, A. M., 18 Oread St., Worcester, Mass.

WHITCOMB, MISS MARY R., Historical Department of Iowa, Des Moines, Iowa.

WHITCOMB, MERRICK, Professor Department of History, University of Cincinnati, Cincinnati, O.

WHITE, ALBERT BEEBE, Ph. D., Assistant Professor of History, University of Minnesota, Minneapolis, Minn.

*WHITE, HON. ANDREW DICKSON, Ph. D., LL. D., D. C. L., Ithaca, N. Y.

WHITE, HENRY ALEXANDER, M. A., Ph. D., D. D., 1800 Senate St., Columbia, S. C.

WHITE, HON. JAY, Ph. B., U. S. Consul, 73 Bodekerstr, Hanover, Germany.

*WHITE, JULIAN LEROY, A. M., 2400 North Ave., West, Baltimore, Md.

*WHITE, HON. PETER, A. M., Marquette, Mich.

WHITEHEAD, HON. JOHN MEEK, A. B., Janesville, Wis.

WHITEHOUSE, H. REMSEN, Villa Denentou, Ouchy, Switzerland.

WHITELEY, HON. JAMES GUSTAVUS, 223 W. Lanvale St., Baltimore, Md.

WHITLEY, REV. W. T., A. M., LL. D., 7 Wolseley Terrace, Preston, England.

WHITNEY, ANNA, A. B., Lock Box 192, Montgomery, Minn.

WHITNEY, ELI, A. M., 800 Whitney Ave., New Haven, Conn.

WHITNEY, GEORGE GILBERT, 826 Dayton Ave., St. Paul, Minn.

WHITNEY, MARY ALICE, A. B., Professor of American History, State Normal School, 827 Market St., Emporia, Kansas.

WHITNEY, SOLON FRANKLIN, A. M., Teacher, Custodian and Librarian of Historical Society, and Librarian of the Free Public Library, Watertown, Mass.

WHITTEMORE, REV. EDWIN C., D. D., Waterville, Me.

WIEHE, CHRISTIAN F., 543 Jackson Boulevard, Chicago, Ill.

WIER, MISS JEANNE ELIZABETH, B. A., Prof. of Hist., University of Nevada; Secretary of Nevada Historical Society, 834 Center St., Reno, Nevada. (Pacific Coast Branch.)

WIGGINS, DR. B. L., Vice-Chancellor University of the South, Sewanee, Tenn.

WIGHT, HON. WILLIAM WARD, A. M., President State Historical Society of Wisconsin, 1020 Wells Building, Milwaukee, Wis.

WILBY, JOSEPH, President Historical and Philosophical Society of Ohio, Burnet Woods Park (604 Neave Bldg.), Cincinnati, Ohio.

WILCOX, MRS. AARON MORLEY, The Arlington Hotel, Washington, D. C.

WILCOX, JENNIE A., 316 Ontario St., Oak Park, Ill.

WILCOX, MISS JESSIE BIRDENA, State Normal School, Ellensburg, Wash. (Pacific Coast Branch.)

WILCOX, WILLIAM CRAIG, A. M., Professor Iowa State University, Iowa City, Iowa.

WILDE, ARTHUR HERBERT, Ph. D., Assistant Professor of History Northwestern University, 2316 Orrington Ave., Evanston, Ill.

WILGUS, JAMES ALVA, M. A., Professor of History and Economics, State Normal School, Platteville, Wis.

WILLARD, JAMES FIELD, Ph. D., 1513 Spruce St., Boulder, Col.

WILLARD, NORMAN P., 1309 Title and Trust Bldg., Chicago, Ill.

WILLIAM JEWELL COLLEGE LIBRARY, Liberty, Mo.

WILLIAMS, ARTHUR, 1 Prospect St., Charlestown, Mass.

WILLIAMS, CHARLES HOWARD, 690 Delaware Ave., Buffalo, N. Y.

WILLIAMS, CHARLES RICHARD, Ph. D., L. H. D., *The News*, Indianapolis, Ind.

WILLIAMS, MISS CORNELIA I. A., 10 Hopper St., Utica, N. Y.

WILLIAMS, FRANCIS, Sheboygan, Wis.

WILLIAMS, FREDERICK M., Box 268, New Milford, Conn.

WILLIAMS, FREDERICK WELLS, 135 Whitney Ave., New Haven, Conn.

WILLIAMS, RT. REV. GERSHOM MOTT, D. D., Marquette, Mich.

WILLIAMS, HENRY SMITH, LL. D., 105 East 19th St., New York, N. Y.

WILLIAMS, TALCOTT, L. H. D., LL. D., Litt. D., 916 Pine St., Philadelphia, Pa.

WILLIAMSON, REV. JAMES D., D. D., 95 Bellflower Ave., Cleveland, Ohio.

WILLIAMSON, OLIVER ROBISON, *The Interior*, McCormack Block, Chicago, Ill.

WILLIS, HENRY, 4036 Baring St., Philadelphia, Pa.

WILLOUGHBY, WESTEL WOODBURY, Ph. D., Associate Professor Johns Hopkins University, Baltimore, Md.

WILMARTH, MRS. MARY JANE, Auditorium Annex, Chicago, Ill.

WILMINGTON INSTITUTE FREE LIBRARY, Wilmington, Del.

WILSEY, FRANK DANE, A. M., 69 West St., New York, N. Y.

WILSON COLLEGE FOR WOMEN, Chambersburg, Pa.

WILSON, EMMA A., State Normal School, Chico, Cal. (Pacific Coast Branch.)

WILSON, GEORGE GRAFTON, Ph. D., Professor Brown University, Providence, R. I.

WILSON, GENERAL JAMES GRANT, D. C. L., President American Ethnological Society, Buckingham Hotel, New York City.

WILSON, DR. J. R., 405 Clay St., Portland, Ore. (Pacific Coast Branch.)

WILSON, MISS JEAN WATSON, B. L., 293 Hurlbut Ave., Detroit, Mich.

WILSON, JESSE B., Lincoln National Bank, Washington, D. C.

WILSON, REV. JOHN A., D. D., LL. D., 230 Fairmount Ave., Pittsburg, Pa.

WILSON, MILTON D., Bartow, Fla.

WILSON, PHILIP SHERIDAN, A. M., Principal Newton Collegiate Institute Newton, N. J.

WILSON, THOMAS, "The Aberdeen," St. Paul, Minn.

WILSON, THOMAS H., First National Bank, 23 Euclid Ave., Cleveland, Ohio.

WILSON, WOODROW, Ph. D., Litt. D., LL. D., President Princeton University, Princeton, N. J.

WILT, JACOB ANDREW, Towanda, Pa.

WING, MISS ELIZABETH, 415 South Commercial St., Nennah, Wis.

WINKLER, ERNEST WILLIAM, B. Litt., A. M., 716 W. 23d St., Austin, Tex.

WINSHIP, GEORGE PARKER, A. M., The John Carter Brown Library, Providence, R. I.

WINSLOW, JOHN BRADLEY, A. M., LL. D., Judge of Supreme Court, Madison, Wis.

*WINSLOW, REV. WILLIAM COPLEY, Ph. D., L. H. D., D. D., LL. D., 525 Beacon St., Boston, Mass.

WINTER, MISS FLORENCE, B. A., Box 72, Southington, Conn.

WINTERBOTHAM, JOHN MILLER, B. L., Madison, Wis.

WIRKLER, JOHN E., 124 Elm St., Oberlin, Ohio.

WIRT, JOHN L., Carnegie Institution, Washington, D. C.

WITHERBEE, HON. FRANK SPENCER, A. M., Port Henry, N. Y.

WITHINGTON, ALBERT LEE, Corresponding Secretary Western Reserve Historical Society, Care Society for Savings, Cleveland, Ohio.

WITHINGTON, LOTHROP, Newburyport, Mass.

WOBURN PUBLIC LIBRARY, Woburn, Mass.

WOLFSON, ARTHUR MAYER, Ph. D., The DeWitt Clinton High School, 59th St. and Tenth Ave., New York, N. Y.

WOLKINS, GEORGE GREGERSON, President Old South Historical Society, 194 Temple St., West Roxbury, Mass.

WOLVERTON, CHARLES EDWIN, Portland, Ore.   (Pacific Coast Branch.)

WOOD, MISS ELIZABETH CORINNE, A. B., A. M., The Wadleigh High School, 114th St. and 7th Ave., New York City.

WOOD, FRANK HOYT, Ph. D., Hamilton College, Clinton, N. Y.

WOOD, MISS LOU, Farmland, Ind.

WOOD, NATHAN SMITH, Saginaw, Mich.

WOODBINE, GEORGE E., B. A., The Elihu Club, 245 York St., New Haven, Conn.

WOODBURN, JAMES ALBERT, Ph. D., Professor Indiana State University, Bloomington, Ind.

WOODCOCK, ABSALOM, Eugene, Ore.   (Pacific Coast Branch.)

WOODMAN, MISS ANNA SOPHIA, A. B., Kent Place School, Snmmit, N. J.

WOODRUFF, GEORGE MORRIS, Litchfield, Conn.

WOODS, HENRY E., A. M., Editor *New England Historical and Genealogical Register* and of Mass. *Vital Records*, 18 Somerset St., Boston, Mass.

WOODWARD, F. A., Wilson, N. C.

WOODWARD, FRANK ERNEST, Secretary Malden Historical Society, Malden, Mass.

WOODWARD, JAMES T., Hanover National Bank, New York.

WOODWARD, P. HENRY, B. A., M. A., President Dime Savings Bank, Vice-President Connecticut General Life Insurance Company, Hartford, Conn.

WOOLLEN, MRS. MARY ALLEN EVANS, 1628 North Pennsylvania St., Indianapolis, Ind.

WOOLSEY, THEODORE SALISBURY, LL. D., Professor Yale University, New Haven, Conn.

WORCESTER FREE PUBLIC LIBRARY, Worcester, Mass.

WRIGHT, HON. CARROLL DAVIDSON, A. M., Ph. D., LL. D., President of Clark College, Worcester, Mass.

WRIGHT, HARRY BURT, Ph. D., 128 York St., New Haven, Conn.

WRIGHT, JAMES M., Johns Hopkins University, P. O. Box 686, Baltimore, Md.

WRIGHT, JOHN HENRY, LL. D., Professor Harvard University, Cambridge, Mass.

WRIGHT, JULIUS TUTWILER, A. M., 933 Dauphin Way, Mobile, Ala.

WRIGHT, RICHARD R., A. M., LL. D., President Georgia State Industrial College, College, Ga.

WRIGHT, ROBERT HERRING, Baltimore City College, Baltimore, Md.

WRONG, GEORGE MCKINNON, A. M., Professor University of Toronto, Toronto, Canada.

WYCHE, BENJAMIN, Librarian, The Carnegie Library, San Antonio, Texas.

WYCKOFF, CHARLES TRUMAN, Ph. D., Professor Bradley Polytecnic Institute, Peoria, Ill.

*YAGER, ARTHUR, Ph. D., President Georgetown College, Georgetown, Ky.

YAGGY, LEVI W., M. S., F. R. G. S., Hutchinson, Kan.

YANCEY, DAVID WALKER, Attorney at Law, Muskogee, Ind. Ter.

YERKES, REV. ROYDEN K., A. B., 5000 Woodland Ave., Philadelphia, Pa.

YORK, LEWIS EDWIN, Superintendent of Schools, Barnesville, Ohio.

YORK, REV. PETER, 1267 16th Ave., Oakland, Cal. (Pacific Coast Branch.)

YOUNG, ALLYN A., Ph. D., Stanford University, Cal.

YOUNG, GEN. BENNETT H., 1535 Fourth Ave., Louisville, Ky.

YOUNG, ELLA, Agnes Scott Academy, Decatur, Ga.

YOUNG, F. G., Professor University of Oregon, Eugene, Oregon. (Pacific Coast Branch.)

YOUNG, GEORGE B., 324 Summit Ave., St. Paul,. Minn.

YOUNG, LEVI EDGAR, B. S., Professor University of Utah, Salt Lake City, Utah.

YOUNG, WALTER STEVENS, B. S., 667 Main St., Worcester, Mass.

YULE, LA MAUDE, Black River Falls, Wis.

ZELIQZON, MAURICE, Ph. D., 4711 Scovill Ave., S. E., Cleveland, Ohio.

ZELLER, PROF. JULIUS CHRISTIAN, 507 E. Chestnut St., Bloomington, Ill.

ZEMBROD, ALFRED CHARLES, M. A., Kentucky University, 456 W. 4th St., Lexington, Ky.

ZESSLER, HELEN, 4936 Champlain Ave., Chicago, Ill.

MEMBERS DECEASED

HONORARY MEMBERS

GARDINER, SAMUEL RAWSON, A. M., Fellow of Merton College, Oxford, England. Died February 24, 1902.

MOMMSEN, THEODOR, Berlin, Germany. Died November 1, 1903.

RANKE, LEOPOLD VON, Berlin, Prussia. Died May 23, 1886.

STUBBS, WILLIAM, Bishop of Oxford, England. Died April 22, 1901.

ADAMS, CHARLES KENDALL, LL. D., Redlands, Cal. Died July 26, 1902.

ADAMS, FRANKLIN G., Secretary Kansas Historical Society, Topeka, Kan. Died December 2, 1899.

*ADAMS, HERBERT BAXTER, Professor Johns Hopkins University, First Vice-President American Historical Association. Died July 30, 1901.

ADAMS, MRS. MARY NEWBURY, Dubuque, Iowa. Died August 5, 1901.

AKINS, THOMAS BEAMISH, D. C. L., Barrister at Law and Commissioner of Public Records of Nova Scotia, Halifax, N. S. Died May 6, 1891.

*ALDEN, MISS MARIA WEED, 12 West 12th St., New York, N. Y. Died ———.

ALDRICH, HON. PELEG EMORY, LL. D., Worcester, Mass. Died March 14, 1895.

*ALGER, HON. RUSSELL ALEXANDER, Detroit, Mich., Died January 24, 1907.

ALLAN, COL. WILLIAM, McDonough P. O., Baltimore Co., Md. Died September 11, 1889.

ALLEN, JEREMIAH MERVIN, M. E., Hartford, Conn. Died December 29, 1903.

ALLEN, WILLIAM FRANCIS, A. M., Professor University of Wisconsin, Madison, Wis. Died December, 9, 1889.

ALLSTON, JOSEPH BLYTH, A. B., Badwell, S. C. Died January 29, 1904.

ANDREWS, ISRAEL WARD, D. D., Professor Marietta College, Marietta, O. Died April 18, 1888.

APPLETON, WILLIAM SUMNER, LL. B., Boston, Mass. Died April 28, 1903.

ARCHIBALD, HON. SIR ADAMS G., D. C. L., K. C. M. G., President Historical Society of Nova Scotia, Halifax, N. S. Died December 15, 1892.

ATHERTON, GEORGE W., President Pennsylvania State College, State College, Pa. Died July 24, 1906.

ATKINSON, EDWARD, Ph. D., LL. D., Box 112, Boston, Mass. Died December 11, 1905.

ATKINSON, WILLIAM PARSONS, A. M., Professor Massachusetts Institute of Technology, Boston, Mass. Died March 10, 1890.

AVERY, SAMUEL PUTNAM, A. M., 4 East 38th St., New York, N. Y. Died August 11, 1904.

BABSON, HON. JOHN JAMES, Gloucester, Mass. Died April 13, 1886.

BAER, DR. H., Charleston, S. C. Died ——.

BAGG, MOSES MEARS, A. M., Librarian Oneida Historical Society, Utica, N. Y. Died May 2, 1900.

BAGLEY, MRS. FRANCES NEWBURY, Detroit, Mich. Died February 7, 1897.

BAIRD, CHARLES WASHINGTON, D. D., Rye, N. Y. Died February 10, 1887.

BAKER, MARCUS, Washington, D. C. Died December 12, 1903.

BAKER, WILLAM SPOHN, Vice-President Pennsylvania Historical Society, Philadelphia, Pa. Died September 10, 1897.

*BALDWIN, HON. CHARLES CANDEE, LL. D., President of Western Reserve Historical Society, Cleveland, O. Died February 2, 1895.

BALDWIN, HENRY, Manzana, Cal. Died January 2, 1905.

BANCROFT, DR. FREDERICK JONES, Denver, Colo. Died 1903.

*BANCROFT, HON. GEORGE, D. C. D., LL. D., Washington, D. C. Died January 17, 1891.

BAXTER, HON. WITTER J., Jonesville, Hillsdale Co., Mich. Died February 6, 1888.

*BAYARD, HON. THOMAS FRANCIS, LL. D., Wilmington, Del. Died September 28, 1898.

BEARDSLEY, EBEN EDWARDS, D. D., LL. D., New Haven, Conn. Died December 21, 1891.

BELKNAP, REAR-ADMIRAL GEORGE EUGENE, LL. D., Boston, Mass. Died April, 1903.

BELL, HON. CHARLES HENRY, LL. D., Exeter, N. H. Died November 11, 1893.

BENNETT, REV. CHARLES WESLEY, Garrett Biblical Institute, Evanston, Ill. Died April 17, 1891.

BERNHEIM, ABRAM C., New York. Died July 24, 1895.

BISSELL, HON. WILSON S., LL. D., Buffalo, N. Y. Died October 6, 1903.

BLAIR, JAMES L., St. Louis, Mo. Died January, 1904.

BLISS, COL. ALEXANDER, Washington, D. C. Died April 30, 1896..

BLISS, CHARLES MILLER, A. M., Bennington, Vt. Died December 21, 1905.

BLISS, WILLIAM ROOT, A. B., Short Hills, N. J. Died April 8, 1906.

BOOTH, HENRY MATTHIAS, D. D., LL. D., President Theological Seminary, Auburn, N. Y. Died March 18, 1899.

BOUTELL, LEWIS HENRY, LL. D., Evanston, Ill. Died January 16, 1899.

BOWMAN, COL. J. B., Little Rock, Ark. Died September 22, 1891.

*BRADLEE, CALEB DAVIS, Ph. D., D. D., Brookline, Mass. Died May 1, 1897.

BRADLEY, WILLIAM H., Chicago, Ill. Died March 1, 1892.

BREVOORT, JAMES CARSON, LL. D., Brooklyn, N. Y. Died December 7, 1887.

BRIGGS, CHARLES C., Pittsburg, Pa. Died July 19, 1901.

BRINTON, DANIEL GARRISON, LL. D., President Numismatic and Antiquarian Society of Philadelphia, Media, Pa. Died July 31, 1899.

BROCK, ROBERT C. H., 1612 Walnut St., Philadelphia, Pa. Died August 8, 1906.

*BRONSON, HENRY, M. D., New Haven, Conn. Died November 26, 1893.

BROOKS, ELDRIDGE STREETER, Vice-President Somerville Historical Society. Died January 7, 1902.

BROOKS, RT. REV. PHILLIPS, D. D., Boston, Mass. Died January 23 1893.

BROWN, COL. JOHN MASON, Louisville, Ky. Died January 29, 1890.

*BROWN, JOHN NICHOLAS, A. M., Providence, R. I. Died May 1, 1900.

BRYMNER, DOUGLAS, LL. D., F. R. S. C., Dominion Archivist, Ottawa, Canada. Died June 19, 1902.

BURTENSHAW, HON. JAMES, Detroit, Mich. Died June 7, 1898.

BUTLER, GEORGE H., M. D., 964 5th Ave., New York, N. Y. Died March 28, 1904.

BYINGTON, EZRA HOYT, Newton, Mass. Died May 16, 1901.

CALDWELL, SAMUEL LUNT, LL. D., Ex-President Vassar College, Providence, R. I. Died September 26, 1889.

CAMPBELL, DOUGLAS, 10 Church St., Schenectady, N. Y. Died March 7, 1893.

CAPEN, ELMER HEWITT, D. D., LL. D., President Tufts College, Tufts College, Mass. Died March 22, 1905.

CARTER, HON. CALVIN HOLMES, Waterbury, Conn. Died September 19, 1887.

CARTER, HON. WALTER STEUBEN, 96 Broadway, New York, N. Y. Died June 3, 1904.

CHAMBERLAIN, HON. MELLEN, LL. D., Chelsea, Mass. Died June 25, 1900.

CHAPLIN, HON. JOHN WAYNE, LL. D., President Michigan State Historical Society, Grand Rapids, Mich. Died July, 1901.

CHILDS, GEORGE WILLIAM, Philadelphia, Pa. Died February 3, 1894.

CLARK, CLARENCE H., 42d and Locust Sts., Philadelphia, Pa. Died March 13, 1906.

CLARK, WALTER, Kamehameha Schools, Honolulu, Hawaii. Died ——

COCKER, HON. WILLIAM JOHNSON, Adrian, Mich. Died May 19, 1901.

*CONELY, HON. EDWIN FORREST, Detroit, Mich. Died April 20, 1902.

COOLEY, HON. THOMAS McINTYRE, LL. D., University of Michigan, Ann Arbor, Mich. Died September 12, 1898.

COTTRELL, ORIN L., Richmond, Va. Died September 5, 1895.

COUDERT, DR. FREDERICK R., 71 Broadway, New York, N. Y. Died December 20, 1903.

COUSAR, HON. ROBERT MOORE, Indian High School, Phœnix, Ariz. Died September, 1903.

*COXE, BRINTON, President Historical Society of Pennsylvania, Philadelphia, Pa. Died September 15, 1892.

CRAMER, MICHAEL JOHN, D. D., LL. D., East Orange, N. J. Died January 23, 1898.

CRANE, MRS. OLIVER, Boston, Mass.

CRUMP, HON. WILLIAM W., Richmond, Va. Died February 27, 1897.

*CULLUM, MAJOR-GENERAL GEORGE W., U. S. A., New York. Died February 28, 1892.

CURRY, HON. JABEZ LAMAR MONROE, LL. D., Washington, D. C. Died February 12, 1903.

CURTIS, GEORGE WILLIAM, L. H. D., LL. D., New Brighton, Staten Island, N. Y. Died August 31, 1892.

DALY, HON. CHARLES PATRICK, LL. D., New York. Died September 19, 1899.

DARLINGTON, GEN. CHARLES WILLIAM, A. M., Corresponding Secretary Oneida Historical Society, Utica, N. Y. Died June 22, 1905.

DAVIES, THOMAS FREDERICK, D. D., LL. D., Detroit, Mich. Died November, 1905.

DAVIS, LEWIS JOHNSON, 1411 Massachusetts Ave., Washington, D. C. Died September 6, 1906.

DAVIS, WILLIAM HENRY, Cincinnati, Ohio. Died ——.

DEANE, CHARLES, LL. D., Vice-President Massachusetts Historical Society, Cambridge, Mass. Died November 13, 1889.

DENNIS, HON. RODNEY STRONG, 148 W. 95th St., New York, N. Y. Died ——.

DETWILER, W. H., Philadelphia, Pa. Died August 31, 1903.

*DE WITT, JOHN E., Portland, Me. Died August 31, 1893.

*DEXTER, HENRY MARTYN, D. D., LL. D., Boston, Mass. Died November 13, 1890.

DODGE, WILLIAM E., 262 Madison Ave., New York, N. Y. Died August 10, 1903.

DUNBAR, CHARLES FRANKLIN, LL. D., Professor Harvard University, Cambridge, Mass. Died January 29, 1900.

EARLE, HON. GEORGE, A. M., LL. D., Washington, D. C. Died May 10, 1899.

EDDY, RICHARD, S. T. D., President of the Universalist Historical Society, Gloucester, Mass. Died ——.

EGGLESTON, EDWARD, L. H. D., Lake George, N. Y. Died September 3 1902.

ELIOT, SAMUEL, LL. D., 44 Brimmer St., Boston, Mass. Died September 14, 1898.

ELLIOTT, WILLIAM HERBERT, Detroit, Mich. Died May 1, 1901.

ELLIS, COL. THOMAS H., Washington, D. C. Died April 11, 1898.

*ELY, HON. HEMAN, Elyria, O. Died July 8, 1894.

ENDICOTT, HON. WILLIAM CROWNINSHIELD, LL. D., Danvers Centre, Mass. Died May 6, 1900.

ENGLISH, HON. WILLIAM HAYDEN, President Indiana Historical Society, Indianapolis, Ind. Died February 7, 1896.

EVARTS, HON. WILLIAM MAXWELL, LL. D., New York. Died February 28, 1901.

FARMER, HON. SILAS, City Historiographer, Detroit, Mich. Died December 28, 1902.

*FIELD, JOHN W., Washington, D. C. Died March 17, 1887.

*FIELD, MARSHALL, Chicago, Ill. Died January 16, 1906.

*FISHER, EUSTACE W., New York. Died March 5, 1894.

*FISH, HON. HAMILTON, LL. D., New York. Died September 7, 1893.

FISKE, PROF. JOHN, Cambridge, Mass. Died July 4, 1901.

FLINT, WESTON, Ph. D., LL. D., "The Cecil," Washington, D. C. Died April 6, 1906.

FOOTE, REV. HENRY WILDER, A. M., Boston, Mass. Died May 29, 1889.

*FORCE, HON. MANNING FERGUSON, LL. D., Sandusky, Ohio. Died May 8, 1899.

FORD, GORDON L., Brooklyn, N. Y. Died November 14, 1891.

FORD, PAUL LEICESTER, 37 East 77th St., New York City. Died May 8, 1902.

FOSTER, ALBERT A., M. D., Marquette, Mich. Died Dec. 6, 1899.

GAMMEL, WILLIAM, LL. D., Professor Brown University, Providence, R. I. Died April 3, 1889.

GANO, JOHN A., Cincinnati, Ohio. Died January 15, 1898.

GARRETT, T. MAURO, Chicago, Ill. Died February 25, 1903.

GARRETT, WILLIAM ROBERTSON, Dean, Peabody College for Teachers, Nashville, Tenn. Died February 12, 1904.

GATES, BEMAN, Marietta, O. Died December 17, 1894.

GAY, SIDNEY HOWARD, West New Brighton, Staten Island, N. Y. Died June 25, 1888.

GOLD, THEODORE SEDGWICK, B. A., M. A., Cream Hill Farm, West Cornwall, Conn. Died March, 1906.

GOODE, GEORGE BROWN, LL. D., Assistant Secretary Smithsonian Institution, Washington, D. C. Died September 6, 1896.

GOODSPEED, GEORGE S., University of Chicago, Chicago, Ill. Died February 17, 1905.

*GRAHAM, ALBERT A., Secretary Ohio Archæological and Historical Society, Columbus, O. Died February 5, 1896.

GREEN, MISS HARRIET ELIZA, Boston Athenæum, Boston, Mass. Died June 26, 1893.

GREENE, COL. JACOB L., A. M., Connecticut Mutual Life Insurance Co., Hartford, Conn. Died March 29, 1905.

*GURNEY, EPHRAIM WHITMAN, A. B., Professor Harvard University, Cambridge, Mass. Died September 12, 1886.

HALE, HON. GEORGE SILSBEE, A. M., Boston, Mass. Died July 27, 1897.

HALSEY, HON. EDMOND D., Morristown, N. J. Died October 17, 1896.

HAMILTON, WILLIAM F., D. D., Washington, Pa. Died March 2, 1899.

HANNA, HON. MARCUS ALONZO, Cleveland, Ohio. Died February 15, 1904.

HARPER, WM. RAINEY, Ph. D., D. D., LL. D., President, University of Chicago, Chicago, Ill. Died January 10, 1906.

HARRISON, HON. HART LYNDE, LL. B., 52 Hillhouse Ave., New Haven, Conn. Died June 8, 1906.

*HASKINS, CHARLES WALDO, L. H. M., Dean of School of Commerce, Accounts and Finance, New York University, 30 Broad St., New York City. Died January 9, 1903.

HASSAM, JOHN TYLER, A. M., Boston, Mass. Died April 22, 1903.

*HAY, HON. JOHN, LL. D., 800 16th St., Lafayette Square, Washington D. C. Died July 1, 1905.

HAYDEN, HON. GEORGE, Ishpeming, Mich. Died July 23, 1902.

HAYES, HON. RUTHERFORD BIRCHARD, LL. D., Frement, O. Died January 17, 1893.

*HAZARD, HON. ROWLAND, A. M., Peace Dale, R. I. Died August 16, 1898.

HEBARD, HON. CHARLES, Chestnut Hill, Philadelphia, Pa. Died June 11, 1902.

HENRY, HON. WILLIAM WIRT, LL. D., Richmond, Va. Died December 5, 1900.

*HEMENWAY, MRS. MARY, Boston, Mass. Died March 6, 1894.

HIGLEY, BREWSTER OWEN, Ph. M., Ohio University, Athens, Ohio. Died April 3, 1905.

HILL, HAMILTON ANDREWS, LL. D., Boston, Mass. Died April 27, 1895.

HINSDALE, BURKE AARON, LL. D., Professor University of Michigan, Ann Arbor, Mich. Died November 29, 1900.

HITCHCOCK, HENRY, LL. D., St. Louis, Mo. Died March 18, 1902.

HOAR, HON. GEORGE FRISBEE, LL. D., Vice-President American Antiquarian Society, Worcester, Mass. Died September 30, 1904.

*HOCKLEY, THOMAS, Philadelphia, Pa. Died March 12, 1892.

HOLT, HON. HENRY HOBART, LL. B., Muskegon, Mich. Died August 23, 1898.

HOMES, HENRY AUGUSTUS, LL. D., Librarian State Library, Albany, N. Y. Died November 3, 1887.

HOPPIN, JAMES MASON, D. D., LL. D., Professor Yale University, New Haven, Conn. Died November 15, 1906.

*HORSFORD, EBEN NORTON, M. D., Professor Harvard University, Cambridge, Mass. Died January 1, 1893.

HUBBARD, GARDINER GREENE, LL. D., Washington, D. C. Died December 11, 1897.

HUBBARD, OLIVER PAYSON, LL. D., Professor Emeritus Dartmouth College, New York City. Died March 9, 1900.

HUBBARD, ROBERT JAMES, Cazenovia, N. Y. Died December 18, 1904.

HUBBARD, LEVERETT M., A. M., LL. B., Wallingford, Conn. Died December, 1906.

HUDSON, JOHN E., Boston, Mass. Died October 1, 1900.

HUTCHINSON, CHARLES HARE, A. M., President of the Athenæum, Philadelphia, Pa. Died in Paris, October, 1902.

INGRAHAM, ANDREW, A. B., Bryant St., Cambridge, Mass. Died August 7, 1905.

ISAACS, JULIEN M., M. S., LL. B., 54 William St., New York, N. Y. Died March 31, 1905.

ISHAM, HON. EDWARD S., LL. D., Chicago, Ill. Died February 16, 1902.

JACOBSON, AUGUSTUS, Union Club, Chicago, Ill. Died October 15, 1903.

JACKSON, D. W., Chicago, Ill. Died January 2, 1897.

JAMES, COL. EDWARD CHRISTOPHER, New York City. Died March 24, 1901.

JAMESON, REV. EPHRAIM ORCUTT, A. B., 5 Chestnut St., Boston, Mass. Died November, 1902.

*JAY, HON. JOHN, LL. D., New York. Died May 5, 1894.

JENKINS, THORNTON ALEXANDER, Rear-Admiral, U. S. N., Washington, D. C. Died August 9, 1893.

JEROME, HON. DAVID H., Saginaw, Mich. Died April 23, 1896.

JOHNSTON, ALEXANDER, LL. D., Princeton, N. J. Died July 20, 1889.

JOHNSTON, HON. JOHN, A. M., LL. D., The Marine National Bank of Milwaukee, Milwaukee, Wis. Died June 1, 1904.

JOHNSTON, WILLIAM PRESTON, LL. D., President Tulane University, New Orleans, La. Died July 16, 1899.

JONES, HON. CHARLES COLCOCK, JR., LL. D., Augusta, Ga. Died July 19, 1893.

JONES, WILLIAM, Providence, R. I. Died March, 1906.

KELLING, HENRY, Walla Walla, Washington. Died July 8, 1895.

KING, HON. HORATIO, LL. D., Washington, D. C. Died May 20, 1897.

*KING, JOHN ALSOP, A. M., President New York Historical Society, Great Neck, Long Island, N. Y. Died November 21, 1900.

KING, J. S., Ouachita College, Arkadelphia, Ark. Died ——.

• KING, HON. RUFUS, LL. D., Cincinnati, O. Died March 25, 1891.

KINGSBURY, FREDERICK JOHN, LL. D., Waterbury, Conn. Died ——.

KIRKLAND, JOSEPH, Chicago. Died April 29, 1894.

KNIGHT, MISS ELIZABETH P., Salem, Mass. Died May 30, 1903.

KNOX, HON. JOHN JAY, New York. Died February 9, 1892.

LACEY, ROWLAND B., President Fairfield County Historical Society, Bridgeport, Conn. Died March 31, 1897.

*LAMB, MRS. MARTHA JOANNA READE, Editor of the *Magazine of American History*, New York. Died January 2, 1893.

*LAMBERT, THOMAS RICKER, D. D., Boston, Mass. Died February 4, 1892.

LAMBORN, ROBERT H., Ph. D., New York. Died January 14, 1895.

LANE, HON. JOHN JAY, A. M., Austin, Texas. Died July —, 1899.

LANGLEY, SAMUEL PIERPONT, D. C. L., LL. D., Secretary Smithsonian Institution, Washington, D. C. Died February 27, 1906.

LATIMER, JAMES F., Ph. D., D. D., Hampden-Sidney, Va. Died February 29, 1892.

LATROBE, HON. JOHN HAZELHURST BONNEVAL, Baltimore, Md. Died September 11, 1891.

LAWRENCE, ABBOTT, A. M., Boston, Mass. Died July 6, 1893.

LAWTON, HON. GEORGE W., Lawton, Mich. Died December 15, 1884.

LEE, HON. HENRY, A. M., Boston, Mass. Died November 24, 1898.

LEITER, LEVI Z., 81 S. Clark St., Chicago., Ill. Died June 9, 1904.

LEWIS, WALTER H., JR., New York. Died November 18, 1899.

LINCOLN, JOHN LARKIN, LL. D., Professor Brown University, Providence, R. I. Died October 17, 1891.

LOGAN, HON. JOHN ALEXANDER, U. S. Senate, Washington, D. C. Died December 26, 1886.

*LOGAN, WALTER SETH, A. M., 27 William St., New York, N. Y. Died July 19, 1906.

LORING, HON. GEORGE BAILEY, M. D., U. S. Minister to Portugal, Washington, D. C. Died September 14, 1891.

LOWELL, EDWARD JACKSON, A. M., Boston, Mass. Died May 11, 1894.

*LOWERY, WOODBURY, A. M., 1621 Pennsylvania Ave., Washington, D. C. Died April 11, 1906.

McCABE, JAMES, Council Bluffs, Iowa. Died May 29, 1902.

McCRADY, EDWARD, LL. D., Vice-President Historical Society of South Carolina, Vice-President American Historical Association, Charleston, S. C. Died November 1, 1903.

McCORMICK, HON. RICHARD C., Jamaica, New York. Died June 2, 1901.

McINTIRE, CLARENCE STANLEY, Ph. D., Philadelphia, Pa. Died August 6, 1900.

*McKINLEY, WILLIAM, President of the United States. Died September 14, 1901.

McMILLAN, HON. JAMES, Detroit, Mich. Died August 10, 1902.

McMILLAN, JAMES HOWARD, A. B., Detroit, Mich. Died May 29, 1902.

McNAUGHTON, DONALD, Albany, N. Y. Died July 30, 1893.

MAGILL, HENRY M., 401 Dodworth Bldg., Pasadena, Cal. Died September 22, 1904.

MARSHALL, WILLIAM L, Principal W. E. Gladstone School, 1882 West 22d St., Chicago, Ill. Died October 30, 1906.

MASON, J. E., Washington, D. C. Died March 4, 1892.

MERRILL, MISS CATHARINE, A. M., Indianapolis, Ind. Died May 30, 1900.

MERRILL, MOSES, 404 Columbia Ave., Boston, Mass. Died April, 1902.

MILLER, JACOB FRANKLIN, Professor in Brigham Young College, Logan, Utah. Died March 25, 1906.

MOOS, BERNARD, Chicago, Ill. Died June 11, 1895.

MORRIS, JONATHAN FLYNT, Treasurer Connecticut Historical Society, Hartford, Conn. Died January 30, 1899.

MORROW, JAMES, D. D., 701 Walnut St., Philadelphia, Pa. Died ——.

*MOWER, MANDEVILLE, New York City. Died.

MOWRY, ARTHUR MAY, A. M., Hyde Park, Mass. Died June 19, 1900.

MURRAY, HON. DAVID, LL. D., New Brunswick, N. J. Died March 6, 1905.

MURRAY, DR. ROBERT DRAKE, Surgeon U. S. Marine Hospital, Key West, Fla. Died Nov. 22, 1903.

MUSSEY, GEN. REUBEN DELEVAN, Washington, D. C. Died May 29, 1892.

NEILL, EDWARD DUFFIELD, D. D., St. Paul, Minn. Died September 26, 1893.

NEWELL, JOHN, Detroit, Mich. Died November, 1885.

*NICOLAY, HON. JOHN GEORGE, Washington, D. C. Died September 26, 1901.

O'HARA, DANIEL J., Toledo, O. Died March 4, 1901.

OLNEY, CHARLES F., 135 Jennings Ave., Cleveland, Ohio. Died July 18, 1903.

ORCUTT, REV. SAMUEL, Bridgeport, Conn. Died January 14, 1893.

OSBORNE, GEORGE STERNE, M. D., North Salem, Mass. Died May 25, 1901.

PACK, ALBERT, Detroit, Mich. Died May 31, 1899.

*PAGE, RICHARD CHANNING MOORE, M. D., New York. Died June 19, 1898.

PAINE, LEVI LEONARD, D. D., Bangor, Me. Died May 10, 1902.

PARKHURST, JOHN GIBSON, Coldwater, Mich. Died April, 1906.

PARKMAN, FRANCIS, LL. D., Vice-President Massachusetts Historical Society, Boston, Mass. Died November 8, 1893.

PARSONS, CHARLES WILLIAM, M. D., Professor Brown University, Providence, R. I. Died September 2, 1893.

PEABODY, HON. CHARLES AUGUSTUS, New York City. Died July 3, 1901.

*PERKINS, AUGUSTUS THORNDIKE, A. M., Boston, Mass. Died April 21, 1891.

PERKINS, SAMUEL CLARKE, LL. D., Philadelphia, Pa. Died July 14, 1903.

PERRY, RT. REV. WILLIAM STEVENS, D. D., LL. D., Bishop of Iowa, Davenport, Iowa. Died May 13, 1898.

PHELAN, HON. JAMES, Ph. D., Memphis, Tenn.   Died January 30, 1891.
*PHILLIPS, HENRY, Jr., A. M., Librarian American Philosophical Society,
    Philadelphia, Pa.   Died June 6, 1895.   •
PIERCE, FREDERICK CLIFTON, Chicago, Ill.   Died April 5, 1904.
PIERCE, PERRY BENJAMIN, A. M., LL. B., Treasurer Anthropological
    Society, 1421 29th St., Washington, D. C.   Died January, 1905.
PLATT, HON. ORVILLE HITCHCOCK, LL. D., U. S. Senate, Washington,
    D. C.   Died April 21, 1905.
POOLE, WILLIAM FREDERICK, LL. D., Librarian Newberry Library, Chi-
    cago, Ill.   Died March 1, 1894.
POORE, MAJOR BENJAMIN PERLEY.   Died May 29, 1887.
POPPLETON, HON. O., President Oakland County Pioneer and Historical
    Society, Birmingham, Mich.   Died March 18, 1892.
*PORTER, REV. EDWARD GRIFFIN, A. M., President New England His-
    toric-Genealogical Society, Dorchester, Mass.   Died February 5,
    1900.
*POSTLETHWAITE, W. M., D. D., Professor U. S. Military Academy, West
    Point, N. Y.   Died January 10, 1896.
POTTER, MRS. E. J. G., 306 Washington Ave., Alpena, Mich.   Died May
    14, 1905.
*PREBLE, REAR-ADMIRAL GEORGE HENRY, U. S. N., Cottage Farm, Mass.
    Died March 1, 1885.
PRENTISS, GEORGE LEWIS, D. D., New York, N. Y.   Died March, 1903.
PULLEN, EUGENE H., New York.   Died April 27, 1899.
PUTNAM, ALFRED PORTER, D. D., President Danvers Historical Society,
    Salem, Mass.   Died April 15, 1906.
PUTNAM, WILLIAM CLEMENT, A. B., 211 Main St., Davenport, Iowa.
    Died January 13, 1906.

RAINES, HON. CADWELL WALTON, Department of Agriculture, Statistics,
    and History, Austin, Texas.   Died August 2, 1906.
RAND, REV. EDWARD A., A. M., Watertown, Mass.   Died October 5, 1903.
RANKIN, REV. JEREMIAH EAMES, LL. D., 1561 Euclid Ave., Cleveland,
    Ohio.   Died November 28, 1904.
*READ, JOHN MEREDITH, A. M., F. S. A., Rue Scribe, Paris, France.
    Died December 27, 1896.
REEVES, ARTHUR M., Richmond, Ind.   Died February 25, 1891.
REYNOLDS, MRS. ANNIE BUCKINGHAM DORRANCE, 29 South River St.,
    Wilkes-Barre, Pa.   Died October 4, 1905.
REYNOLDS, SHELDON, President Wyoming Historical and Geological
    Society, Wilkes-Barre, Pa.   Died February 8, 1895.

RICE, HON. ALEXANDER HAMILTON, LL. D., Boston, Mass. Died July 22, 1895.

RICE, WILLIAM, Public Library, Springfield, Mass. Died August 17, 1897.

RICHARDS, JEREMIAH, 352 West 87th St., New York, N. Y. Died June, 1906.

RICKETSON, HON. JOHN HOWLAND, A. M., Allegheny, Pa. Died July 20, 1900.

*RIVES, WILLIAM CABELL, LL. B., Newport, R. I. Died April 7, 1889.

ROBERTS, CHARLES, A. B., 1716 Arch St., Philadelphia, Pa. Died January 23, 1902.

ROBERTSON, RT. REV. C. F., D. D., LL. D., Bishop of Missouri, St. Louis, Mo. Died May 1, 1886.

ROCKWELL, GEN. ALFRED PERKINS, A. M., Ph. B., 281 Beacon St., Boston, Mass. Died ——.

ROCKWOOD, CHARLES GREENE, 70 So. 11th St., Newark, N. J. Died July 17, 1904.

ROPES, JOHN CODMAN, LL. D., Boston, Mass. Died October 28, 1899.

ROWLAND, WILLIAM LEONARD, Rockford, Ill. Died September 27, 1900.

SALISBURY, EDWARD ELBRIDGE, LL. D., New Haven, Conn. Died February 5, 1901.

SALTONTALL, HON. LEVERETT, A. M., Collector of the Port of Boston and Charlestown, Boston, Mass. Died April 15, 1895.

SAUNDERS, HON. WILLIAM LAWRENCE, LL. D., Secretary of State, Raleigh, N. C. Died April 2, 1891.

*SCHAFF, REV. PHILIP, D. D., LL. D., New York. Died October 20, 1893.

SCHUYLER, HON. EUGENE, LL. D. Died at Venice, Italy, July 16, 1890.

SCHUYLER, HON. GEORGE WASHINGTON, Ithaca, N. Y. Died February 1, 1888.

SCOTT, GEORGE ROBERT WHITE, D. D., Newton, Mass. Died September 13, 1902.

*SCOTT, LEWIS ALLAIRE, A. B., Vice-President Numismatic and Antiquarian Society, Philadelphia, Pa. Died August 11, 1896.

SCOTT, WILLIAM 450 4th Ave., Pittsburgh, Pa. Died February 27, 1906.

SCRIPPS, JAMES EDMUND, *The Evening News*, Detroit, Mich. Died ——.

SCUDDER, HORCE ELISHA, Litt. D., Cambridge, Mass. Died January 11, 1902.

SEISS, JOSEPH AUGUSTUS, D. D., LL. D., L. H. D., President Lutheran Theological Seminary, Philadelphia, Pa. Died June 20, 1904.

SESSIONS, F. C., President State Historical Society, Columbus, Ohio. Died March 26, 1892.

Sheaffer, P. W., Pottsville, Pa. Died March 26, 1891.

*Shearer, Hon. James, Bay City, Mich. Died October 14, 1896.

Shoemaker, Col. M., Jackson, Mich. Died November 10, 1895.

Shorey, Hon. Daniel Lewis, A. B., Chicago, Ill. Died March 4, 1899.

Sill, John M. B., Detroit, Mich. Died April 6, 1901.

*Skinner, Hon. Mark, Chicago, Ill. Died September 16, 1887.

Smith, Edward Payson, Ph. D., Worcester, Mass. Died May 2, 1892.

Smith, Gen. George William, Chicago, Ill. Died September, 1898.

Smith, Judson, D. D., 14 Beacon St., Boston, Mass. Died June 29, 1906.

Smith, Thomas Watson, D. D., 72 Robie St., Halifax, N. S. Died March 8, 1902.

Smith, William Henry, Lake Forest, Ill. Died July 27, 1896.

Smyth, Egbert Coffin, D. D., Andover, Mass. Died April 12, 1904.

Snow, Hon. Freeman, Ph. D., Harvard University, Cambridge, Mass. Died September 12, 1894.

Soule, Miss Annah May, M. L., Mt. Holyoke College, South Hadley, Mass. Died March 7, 1905.

Speed, Capt. Thomas, Custom House, Louisville, Ky. Died January 31, 1905.

Speer, Charles Edward, Pittsburgh, Pa. Died May 2, 1905.

Stevens, Benjamin Franklin, L, H. D., F. S. A., London, England. Died March 5, 1902.

Stille, Charles Janeway, LL. D., President Historical Society of Pennsylvania, Philadelphia, Pa. Died August 11, 1899.

Stockbridge, Hon. Henry, Baltimore, Md. Died March 11, 1895.

Stone, Carl August, A. M., Professor Bethany College, Lindsborg, Kansas. Died June 5, 1898.

Storrs, Richard Salter, D. D., LL. D., Brooklyn, N. Y. Died June 5, 1900.

Stryker, Gen. William Scudder, A. M., LL. D., President New Jersey Historical Society, Trenton, N. J. Died October 29, 1900.

Swensson, Carl Aaron, Ph. D., D. D., President, Bethany College, Lindsborg, Kan. Died February 16, 1904.

Terrett, William Rogers, D. D., Hamilton College, Clinton, N. Y. Died May 4, 1902.

Thomas, John H., D. D., Oxford, Ohio. Died January, 1904.

Thomas, Joseph, LL. D., Philadelphia, Pa. Died December, 1891.

Thurber, Hon. Henry T., Detroit, Mich. Died March 16, 1904.

Thurston, Robert Henry, A. M., LL. D., Professor Sibley College, Cornell University, Ithaca, N. Y. Died Oct. 25, 1903.

TILLMAN, MRS. WALTER P., 40 First St., Troy, N. Y. Died December, 1904.

TONER, JOSEPH MEREDITH, Library of Congress, Washington, D. C. Died July 30, 1896.

TOPPAN, ROBERT NOXON, A. M., Corresponding Secretary Prince Society, Cambridge, Mass. Died May 10, 1901.

TORREY, HENRY WARREN, LL. D., Professor Harvard University, Cambridge, Mass. Died December 14, 1893.

TOWNSEND, GEN. EDWARD DAVIS, U. S. A., Washington, D. C. Died May 10, 1893.

TROWBRIDGE, THOMAS R., Corresponding Secretary New Haven Colony Historical Society, New Haven, Conn. Died October 25, 1898.

TRUMBULL, HON. JAMES HAMMOND, LL. D., Secretary for Foreign Correspondence American Antiquarian Society, Hartford, Conn. Died August 5, 1897.

TUTTLE, HERBERT, L. H. D., Professor Cornell University, Ithaca, N. Y. Died June 22, 1894.

*TYLER, MOSES COIT, L. H. D., LL. D., Professor Cornell University, Ithaca, N. Y. Died December 28, 1900.

UNDERWOOD, HAROLD GREEN, LL. B., 107 Wisconsin St., Milwaukee, Wis. Died May 12, 1905.

*UPHAM, WILLIAM PHINEHAS, A. B., Newtonville, Mass. Died——

WAITE, HON. MORRISON REMICK, LL. D., Chief Justice of the United States, Washington, D. C. Died March 23, 1888.

*WALKER, FRANCIS AMASA, LL. D., President Massachusetts Institute of Technology, Boston, Mass. Died January 5, 1897.

WARREN, WILLIAM WILKINS, Boston, Mass. Died January 23, 1890.

WATERMAN, C. A., Hot Springs, Neb. Died December 13, 1904.

WEAVER, GERRIT ELIAS HAMBLETON, A. M., 916 Farragut Terrace, Philadelphia, Pa. Died February 21, 1904.

WEEKES, JOHN ABELL, New York. Died May 23, 1901.

*WELLING, JAMES C., LL. D., President Columbian University, Washington, D. C. Died September 4, 1894.

WHEELER, N. M., Professor University of Southern California, Los Angeles, Cal. Died December 5, 1886.

*WHEELWRIGHT, EDWARD, A. M., President The Colonial Society of Boston, Mass., Boston, Mass. Died May 9, 1900.

WHEILDON, WILLIAM WILLDER, Concord, Mass. Died January 7, 1892.

WHITAKER, HERSCHEL, Secretary American Fisheries Society, Detroit, Mich. Died May 5, 1900.

CPSIA information can be obtained
at www.ICGtesting.com
Printed in the USA
BVHW04*1111100918
527043BV00010B/431/P